Television Dialogue

Studies in Corpus Linguistics (SCL)

SCL focuses on the use of corpora throughout language study, the development of a quantitative approach to linguistics, the design and use of new tools for processing language texts, and the theoretical implications of a data-rich discipline.

Volume 36

Television Dialogue. The sitcom *Friends* vs. natural conversation
by Paulo Quaglio

Television Dialogue

The sitcom *Friends* vs. natural conversation

Paulo Quaglio

State University of New York at Cortland

John Benjamins Publishing Company

Amsterdam / Philadelphia

™ The paper used in this publication meets the minimum requirements of
American National Standard for Information Sciences – Permanence of
Paper for Printed Library Materials, ANSI z39.48-1984.

Library of Congress Cataloging-in-Publication Data

Quaglio, Paulo.
  Television dialogue : the sitcom Friends vs. natural conversation / by Paulo Quaglio.
       p. cm. (Studies in Corpus Linguistics, ISSN 1388-0373 ; v. 36)
  Includes bibliographical references and index.
  1. Dialogue analysis. 2. Conversation analysis. 3. Friends (Television program) I. Title.
  P95.455.Q34   2009
  302.3'46--dc22   2008048558
  ISBN 978 90 272 2310 4 (HB; alk. paper)
  ISBN 978 90 272 2316 6 (PB; alk. paper)
  ISBN 978 90 272 9044 1 (EB)

John Benjamins Publishing Co. · P.O. Box 36224 · 1020 ME Amsterdam · The Netherlands
John Benjamins North America · P.O. Box 27519 · Philadelphia PA 19118-0519 · USA

Table of contents

List of tables

List of figures

Foreword

Douglas Biber

Don't we talk just like people on television? Or rather, don't those people talk just like us? Conversations on television seem completely natural to the normal viewer. But is that because we have come to expect a particular style of interaction on TV, or because those interactions accurately capture the actual linguistic characteristics of everyday conversation?

Corpus-based analysis is ideally suited for a research question of this type, and that is exactly what Paulo Quaglio offers us in the present book. The corpus analyzed here comprises transcripts of episodes from one of the most popular TV sitcoms – *Friends* – which is compared to a large corpus of normal face-to-face conversations.

By using sophisticated corpus analysis techniques, Quaglio is able to undertake a comprehensive lexico-grammatical description of TV dialogue in this popular sitcom, in comparison to the linguistic characteristics of everyday conversation. The result is probably the most thorough linguistic description of television interactive discourse accomplished to date.

The general linguistic survey is complemented by more in-depth chapters that focus on particular distinctive aspects of TV discourse, including vague language, the expression of personal emotion, informal language (including slang and expletives), and a comparison of narrative features in *Friends* versus natural conversation.

In conclusion, Quaglio tackles the pedagogical implications of this research, asking whether the linguistic patterns found in TV discourse provide a suitable model for language learners. Taken together, this study will be of interest to a wide range of readers, including scholars interested in conversation and discourse analysis, media scholars, applied linguists, and corpus linguists generally.

CHAPTER 1

Opening credits
Conversation and TV dialogue

1.1 Introduction: What this book is about

In a nutshell, this book reports on a linguistic study comparing the language of a popular American television situation comedy, *Friends*, to natural conversation. What is it that makes scripted dialogue *sound* natural or contrived? Is television dialogue expected or meant to sound like naturally-occurring conversation? Whether the intention is to write dialogues that resemble natural conversation as closely as possible or to purposely diverge from authentic talk, one has to be aware of the rules governing conversation. In other words, knowledge of the linguistic choices speakers make and what these choices reflect functionally is essential whether the purpose is to follow or break these rules. Consider the following excerpts from *Friends* and natural conversation:

> Excerpt 1:
> Phoebe: Hey Rach, what time do you get off? We're all gonna do something tonight.
> Rachel: Umm.... well, actually I'm already done, but I...I <u>kinda</u> got plans. (*Friends*)

> Excerpt 2:
> A: Yeah. So is it okay if I take a look at those pictures?
> B: Well I <u>kind of</u> have to leave them right now. (Conversation)

In terms of 'informational content', Rachel's turn could have been *I got plans*; by the same token, speaker B's utterance could have been *I have to leave them right now*. Why did the speakers choose to add the hedge *kind of/kinda* to their utterances? What is the functional effect of this addition? Did you notice that both started with the discourse marker *well*?

Notice the use of the hedge *kind of like* in the next excerpt from conversation. Does it have the same effect of *kind of* above? Does it add a degree of imprecision to the utterance? If so, does it seem to hinder comprehension and thus negatively impact the dynamic of the communicative event? Would it make sense to say that this apparent imprecision actually adds to the interactiveness of the dialogue?

Excerpt 3:

A: It's <u>kind of like</u> a dialysis machine. And all of your blood goes out of your right arm and it goes into this thing that goes around and around, I can never remember the word for it.

B: Centrifuge?

A: A centrifuge.

B: And it washes the blood.

A: And the blood plasma goes out where all the bad shit stays in

B: Uh huh. (Conversation)

The tone of conversational exchanges is also created through or reflected by the use of linguistic devices. Obviously, the volume of voice, intonation patterns, speech rate as well as nonverbal elements such as gestures and facial expressions reflect the tone of the conversation. What if all of these telling clues were stripped off the dialogue? Could we still perceive the tone of the interaction and intentions of the speakers? Consider Excerpt 4 below from *Friends*. What is the tone of the exchanges? Friendly, Rude, Emotional? The use of certain linguistic features, such as adverbial intensifiers *really* and *so*, (mild) expletive *sucks*, the three instances of the discourse marker *Oh*, and the emphatic *even* reveal much of the emotional tone of the exchanges.

Excerpt 4:

Monica: Hey Phoebe... how you doin'? You feelin' better?

Phoebe: Breaking up <u>sucks</u>! <u>Oh</u>, I really miss Mike!

Chandler: <u>Oh</u>, I'm <u>so</u> sorry!

Phoebe: <u>Oh</u> God, I tried everything to make myself feel better. I <u>even</u> tried writing a song about it... (*Friends*)

The speakers in Excerpt 5 are having a 'philosophical' discussion about a movie and one of the actors' performances in particular. This dialogue has numerous linguistic features reflecting the tone of the interaction. Does the expletive *shit* reflect a confrontational atmosphere between the interlocutors? What kind of information can be gleaned from the use of the vocatives *dude* and *man*? How about the innovative use of *totally* as an expression of agreement?

Excerpt 5:

A: He's like incredibly present and you can see it all over his face and it's like, and everything, it's like when you're on acid basically. Except like you know, that part of acid except like in a sober controlled another way.

B: Yeah.

A: But that element of it.

B: Right.

A: There's a lot when you're tripping, a lot of other <u>shit</u> happening. But that particular element of that like super presence. Like I'm so aware of everything around me. It's like, you know

B: Yeah <u>totally</u>. <u>Dude</u> I think I had to bail like a long time ago.

A: Yeah <u>man</u> you definitely should. (Conversation)

The excerpts above illustrate some of the many linguistic features that characterize natural conversation and some of the functional issues involving the choice of grammatical features speakers make to accomplish different communicative goals. These linguistic features and their functional correlates are the basis for the comparison of the language of the dialogues in *Friends* to naturally-occurring conversation in the present study.

1.2 What this book is not about

Because conversation is interactive, speakers are often eager to participate in the communicative event. This cooperation often results in overlaps, interruptions, and incomplete utterances without interfering much with the flow of the exchanges. The virtual absence of these features in television dialogue is probably one of the most salient differences between the two registers. Consider Excerpt 6 from conversation, for example. Notice that speaker C is interrupted and does not complete his utterance. Not surprisingly, one of the most frequent 'collocates' of overlaps is the notation *<unclear>*, indicating that the transcriber was unable to understand the utterance. In the first five turns of this dialogue excerpt, [signed] and [Hadn't he already signed a form?] overlap with [<unclear>].

<u>Excerpt 6</u>:

(Note: [ ] Square brackets indicate overlap.)

A: [I thought he] had already [signed.]

B: [<unclear>]

?: Okay

B: [<unclear> batteries.]

A: [Hadn't he already signed a form?]

B: [He already signed it]

A: [And then he decided to] change his mind?

B: And then he came [stomping into the room]

C: [He] said something that he didn't] want...

B: Well, that could be but right after you left I went to collect all the blue forms, they were filling them out and... (Conversation)

The overlaps exemplified above do not seem to have hindered comprehension. Even if they had interfered with comprehension, the interlocutors could have asked clarification questions to remedy the situation. If this characteristic of conversation were to be portrayed in television dialogue, comprehension would certainly be hindered. These discourse features of conversation certainly deserve to be analyzed but are beyond the scope of the present study.

Also important especially in sociolinguistically-oriented conversation studies but beyond the scope of the present study are the roles of gender and social status in the grammatical choices speakers make. I also acknowledge the importance of pragmatics; numerous studies have contributed much to our understanding of conversation from this perspective. A comparison between *Friends* and conversation from the standpoint of pragmatics would be another interesting study, especially because humor seems to be often created through pragmatic failure. However, even though I comment on the influence of humor on the choice of some linguistic features in *Friends*, I do not focus on this aspect of conversation. Hopefully, this study will inspire other researchers to tackle the analysis of television dialogue from several different viewpoints.

I wish to emphasize that the primary purpose of this book is not to provide an in-depth description and discussion of natural conversation. The aim of the present study is to compare high-frequency linguistic features that characterize conversation to the language of *Friends*. As a natural offshoot of this comparison, this book provides a description and analysis of a large number of conversational features. It should be noted, however, that this is not a study primarily focused on conversation. As such, several potentially interesting conversational features were not included in the study for practical reasons or because their analysis was beyond the scope of the study (see Chapter 3, Section 3.8 for the rationale underlying the choice of linguistic features).

Finally, it is not my intention to provide a detailed discussion of competing terminology of conversational features. For example, *discourse markers* (e.g., *well, you know, wow*) have received a great deal of research attention and have been labeled and defined in several different ways according to their form and discourse function. For the purposes of this study, I provide a simple operational definition and 'supplement' it with several examples from *Friends* and conversation. In addition, I direct the reader to other pertinent studies that have examined the feature in more detail.

1.3 Conversation studies

Conversation has been analyzed from several different yet complementary perspectives. For example, much contribution to our understanding of conversation has been made by scholars in conversation analysis (e.g., Ford, Fox, & Thompson, 2002 on turn-taking; Schegloff & Sacks, 1973 on adjacency pairs; Wong, 2000a on repair). Pragmatics has also been a very productive area of enquiry with topics as diverse as speech acts (e.g., Sbisa, 2002), implicature (e.g., Grice, 1975, 1989), conversational relevance (e.g., Wilson & Sperber, 2002), and politeness (e.g., Bargiela-Chiappini, 2003) to mention just a few. Also focusing on pragmatic concerns, much research has been carried out from a descriptive standpoint. These studies have addressed a wide range of topics, such as discourse markers (e.g., Schiffrin, 1987), formulaic expressions (e.g., Ward & Birner, 1993), and conversational routines and phraseology (Coulmas, 1981).

Despite the great deal of research interest in conversation, not much emphasis has been placed on large-scale grammatical descriptions of conversation (Quaglio & Biber, 2006).[1] Comprehensive comparisons between conversation and other conversational registers from a strictly grammatical perspective are even rarer.

In all of the excerpts shown in Section 1.1, the linguistic choices made by the speakers are not arbitrary; rather, they reflect the 'discourse circumstances of conversation.' The *Longman Grammar of Spoken and Written English* (Biber et al.,1999) (henceforth LGSWE) devotes a whole chapter (Chapter 14) to the *grammar of conversation*, discussing the relationship between the discourse circumstances of conversation (e.g., real-time production, shared context, interactiveness) and the grammatical features that reflect these circumstances, thus typifying naturally- occurring conversation. Much of the selection of linguistic features in the present study is based on a survey of LGSWE, which presents descriptions and analyses of grammatical features based on a comprehensive corpus-based study involving four registers: academic writing, news reportage, fiction, and conversation. In the next section, I present a brief summary of the relationship between the structural and functional correlates of conversational features discussed in Chapter 14 of LGSWE, *The Grammar of Conversation*, which, in large part, provided the framework for the present study. In order to not 'clutter' this brief outline with definitions and references, I just label the linguistic features and provide examples. All of these features will be described and discussed later in the book in the specific chapters they are addressed.

---

1.   But see Rühlemann (2007) for an excellent analysis of numerous conversational features within a situational framework.

1.3.1 The discourse circumstances of conversation

Even though the discourse circumstances of conversation are presented separately for ease of comprehension, analysis, and exemplification, they are intrinsically related. For example, the fact that conversation has a high frequency of reductions (e.g., ellipsis, substitute pro-forms) reflects not only the shared context in which conversation takes place but also its interactive nature, as unnecessary elements may slow down the communicative process. However, some linguistic features seem to be *primarily* associated with one of these situations and are thus described here in this fashion. It should also be noted that because particular features often have different functions depending on the context, they may be described in this brief summary as associated with different situations than those highlighted in LGSWE.

Conversation takes place in shared context. Interactions involve not only awareness of the surrounding physical context but also background knowledge, which often includes personal information shared only by the interlocutors. For this reason, the analysis of conversation corpora can be challenging at times due to lack of this contextual and situational information.

Some of the linguistic features that reflect shared context are: first- and second-person pronouns, ellipses, substitute pro-forms (e.g., *one/ones, do it/that*), and deictic expressions (e.g., *this, that*). In example (1), the speakers are talking about how a piano was taken out of one of the speakers' house. In addition to the several instances of personal pronouns *I* and *you*, the excerpt below has a deictic item in *got that out of the house*, which later is made explicit by speaker B (grand piano), and an example of a substitute pro-form, *do it*. Access to the background knowledge (the fact that speaker A and his wife Nancy took the grand piano out of their house) is obviously shared by both speakers, making this omitted item easily retrievable.

(1) A: <u>You</u> and Nancy took it out, didn't <u>you</u>? <u>I</u> often wondered how <u>you</u> ever got <u>that</u> out of the house.

B: We rented a dolly and we took the legs off and stood it up just, <u>I</u> mean, the guy at this music store told us just how to <u>do it</u> and <u>I</u> went to a music store and said how do <u>you</u> move a grand piano?

Example (2) illustrates two cases of ellipsis. Speaker A omits the auxiliary verb *are*; this type of ellipsis occurs in unstressed positions. Speaker B provides only new information (a cheeseburger), avoiding the repetition of the whole clause, *I'm gonna order a cheeseburger*. Due to the shared context, the repetition of the whole clause becomes cumbersome and unnecessary. Ultimately, these omissions speed up the communicative event, thus reflecting the dynamic, interactive nature of conversation.

(2) A: What < > you gonna order, Bry?

   B: < > a cheeseburger.

Conversation avoids elaboration of meaning. Also because speakers rely on shared context, they avoid specification of meaning, giving conversation an apparent imprecision quality. Among other features, this lack of elaboration is reflected in the high frequency of conversational hedges (e.g., *sort of, kind of*), nouns of vague reference (e.g., *thing, stuff*), and vague coordination tags (e.g., *or something, stuff like that*). These 'vague devices' can have different functions in different contexts.

(3) A: I wonder if there's some <u>sort of</u> building code.

   B: There might be. I don't know. Okay, there's also a comforter in the back seat?

(4)   … I don't want to get into <nv_laugh>all this <u>stuff</u> about what did he really mean when he said this or that 'cause people spend too much time I think arguing about that…

(5) A: <unclear> something this weekend?

   B: Maybe, if you call, whatever

   A: If you want to check out that shrine on Sunday <u>or something</u>

   B: Yeah, that would be cool

In (3), speaker A's reference to *some sort of building code* suggests his awareness that *building code* might not be the most appropriate term to express the intended meaning. However, had speaker A tried to be more precise, it would probably have taken him longer to produce this turn and would thus have slowed down the communicative process. In addition, this is also a way of involving the interlocutor in the creation of meaning, which, obviously, is understood due to the shared context. Similarly, in (4) the speaker avoids repeating information shared by the interlocutor. As such, *stuff*, a 'noun of vague reference,' provides the core information needed by the interlocutor. Finally, in (5) the coordination tag *or something* is instrumental in making speaker's A utterance less direct or imposing, adding an element of flexibility to the invitation.

Conversation takes place in real time. The natural pressures of online communication give speakers very little time to plan or edit their utterances. The use of nouns of vague reference and hedges, discussed above, is also related to the pressures of online production. In the attempt to not truncate the conversation, speakers become 'less precise.'

Perhaps the most salient result of real-time production is the presence of hesitations, repeats, and incomplete sentences. These features, all of which illustrated in (7), reflect the lack of time for planning and editing which characterizes conversation. Hesitators (often referred to as *filled pauses*) are often used to fill the potential vacuum brought about by pauses (especially longer pauses). As Wardhaugh (1985) points out, at times "silence during a conversation creates…embarrassment to the participants…because [it] signals a failure to keep alive what the participants regard as this essentially cooperative venture" (pp. 49–50). Discourse markers such as *you know* can be extremely functional in conversation: they not only help fill the potential void that pauses may leave, but also allow time for speakers to organize their thoughts before verbalizing them. Further, they can be instrumental in helping speakers 'hold the floor.' In (8), *you know* seems to be a natural extension of the hesitator *um*; the hedge *kind of* sends the message that perhaps *out of control* is not the most adequate way of describing the situation, but because of lack of time to come up with a better explanation, the speaker transfers the responsibility of creating meaning to his interlocutor.

(7)   A   I haven't done the any of *the the* {repeat} follow thank you stuff to Janet <name> *um* {hesitator}and that was *I I* {repeat} just had that on my list to do because *um*… {hesitator}want to finalize the date for that other stuff, but that needs to be copied to whole slew of people <unclear>

    B: Speaking of Janet <name> you know something, I still don't have <unclear> videos for front of <unclear>. I mean if she {incomplete sentence}

    A: Did he give it to you?

(8)   … Let's do what other magazines do. <u>Um</u>, <u>you know</u>, so that just got <u>kind of</u> out of control…

Conversation is interactive. Nonclausal units are a typical result of the pressures of online production but also reveal the interactive nature of conversation. They include some discourse markers (e.g., *well*), single-word responses (e.g., *okay*, *wow*), ellipsis, and polite formulas. Example (9) contains all of these features. Similar to pauses and the discourse marker *you know* mentioned above, the discourse marker *well* is often used as a way of avoiding pauses while speakers organize their thoughts without 'losing the floor.' The single-word response *Okay* can be indicative of interest, agreement, or comprehension. *I wish you good luck* is reduced to simply *good luck*, being faster and more efficient than the clausal unit. The same simplification occurs with *thanks*, which takes the place of the clausal *I thank you*.

(9)   A: <u>Well</u> let's see, tonight should be much more active I think.
    B: <u>Well</u> let me be off on my little rounds.
    A: <u>Okay</u>.

B: <u>Good luck</u> with the survey.

A: <u>Thanks</u>.

Conversation expresses stance. Especially in casual conversation, speakers often express their feelings, opinions, and evaluations. In addition to high frequencies of evaluative adjectives (e.g., *beautiful, interesting, boring*), features such as stance adverbs (e.g., *actually, really, probably*) and *that*-complement clauses controlled by mental verbs (e.g., *think, know*) are very frequent. *Probably* indicates doubt; *really* and *actually* can have different pragmatic functions depending on intonation, tone of voice, and even nonverbal clues (e.g., facial expression). Example (10) has a *that*-complement clause (deleted) controlled by *think* and then followed by *actually*. Notice that here *actually* seems to have a buffering effect as speaker B presents a different fact than that suggested by speaker A, thus either mitigating the effect of a direct contradiction or, perhaps, highlighting the contradiction. The two instances of the discourse marker *Oh* can signal surprise, disbelief, or even indignation depending on intonation and tone of voice.

(10) A: Well isn't Jeanette sort of, she's gonna be adopting as a single person. Right?

B: Uh huh. I <u>think</u> Ann is <u>actually</u> doing adoption.

C: Yeah.

A: <u>Oh</u>. <u>Oh</u>.

Conversational exchanges can be emotionally loaded. Adverbial intensifiers (e.g., *really, so*), interjections (e.g., *wow, really*), and expletives can be instrumental in the expression of emotion. In (11), speaker B expresses surprise with an exclamatory utterance that includes the interjection *Wow* and the intensifier *really*. Even without prosodic information in (12), it is clear that the exchange is rather emotional; the presence of linguistic features such as the expletives *shit* and *fucking* and the adverbial intensifier *really* makes the tone of the conversation evident. Notice that the evaluative adjective *bad* is intensified not only by *really* but also by *that*; the choice of *shit hole* to qualify the place where apparently both speakers live clearly evidences speaker A's dissatisfaction with the current living arrangements; interestingly, *fucking*, which usually intensifies an adjective (e.g., *fucking bad*), affects the whole proposition, as it reveals speaker A's overall state of mind.

(11) A: Now, that's something we looked at before.

B: <u>Wow</u>, it looks <u>really</u> different now.

A: Uh, huh.

(12) A: It's seven more months until we move out of this <u>shit hole</u>.

B: Yeah, into lovely beautiful downtown Albuquerque.

A: Is it <u>really</u> that bad?

B: It's horrible.

A: Please don't <u>fucking</u> say that, Cooper. You realize it's my only option, I have no other options.

With this brief overview of the 'discourse circumstances of conversation' (LGSWE, Chapter 14), I hope to have provided the reader with a flavor of the nature of the analysis presented in this book. In the next section, I present an overview of television studies in general and television dialogue in particular.

1.4 Television studies

Television has been the object of scholarly work from several different perspectives. For example, there has been a plethora of studies on sociocultural aspects regarding television news broadcast (e.g., Adoni, Cohen, & Mane, 1984; Cohen, Adoni, & Bantz, 1990), ideological issues (e.g., Fiske, 1987; Lembo, 2000; Morley, 1994), the depiction of violence in prime time (e.g., Potter & Smith, 2000; Signorielli, 2003), and sexuality issues (e.g., Battles & Morrow-Hilton, 2002).

Television talk shows (e.g., *The Jerry Springer Show*, *The Oprah Winfrey Show*) have been the object of several studies. Even though most of them focus on cultural/social issues (e.g., Davis & Mares, 1998; Grabe, 2002; Woo & Dominick, 2001), naturally-occurring data are analyzed in some of these studies of broadcast talk, using methodologies from sociolinguistics, conversation analysis, and pragmatics. These studies focus on issues, such as models of daytime talk shows (Haarman, 2001), debate/conflict management (Wood, 2001), and the creation of conflict (Myers, 2001). As Tolson (2001) points out, however, the language of talk shows, "unlike ordinary conversation … must be understood as 'institutional;' that is 'talk' produced in an institutional setting… produced for, and oriented toward, an overhearing audience…" (p. 28).

1.4.1 Television dialogue

Several 'manuals' on how to write dialogue for television are commercially available. Virtually no linguistic information is provided in these manuals; most 'tips' rely on native-speaker intuition. Smith (1999) says that "dialogue should be written in a conversational style" (p. 148) and comments on the issue of language appropriateness by stating that age, education, and cultural background of the characters should be taken into account. However, no linguistic information regarding the features that characterize 'conversational style' is provided. Even though

Cooper (1997) addresses the issue of audience identification by pointing out that the characters address four basic audience needs (i.e., universal emotions, new information, conflict resolution, and completion), nothing is said about how these needs are linguistically realized by the characters. The author limits his comments by saying that "characters ... express emotions that provoke a sense of recognition in viewers" (p. 91).

Some authors recognize the importance of observing naturally-occurring conversation as a model for good dialogue writing. Hunter (1994) states that "just as you need the eye to see, you also need the ear to hear and overhear ... real people talk for dialogue, stories, and scenes" (p. 28). Horton (1999) suggests taping naturally-occurring conversation in order to "study ... how people talk, respond, choose their words, make their delivery" (p. 141).

DiMaggio (1990) makes insightful comments as she discusses the time restrictions imposed by the televised medium on dialogue writing: "a teleplay is the bare necessities, the bones, the skeleton; it is the blueprint of visuals of fragments that give the *illusion* of a complete story" (p. 32). Earlier the author had noted that

> When you read television scripts ... you will be amazed at how simple they appear. This simplicity is an illusion simply because in good scripts the writing is so economical. Television is a *visual* art form ... To write for television, you must think in pictures. (p. 11)

Even though this comment was on the time limitations of television, the author is, perhaps unintentionally, making reference to a crucial difference between the written and spoken mode. The visual aspect of television and its ensuing economical language are chiefly related to some of the discourse circumstances of conversation described in the previous section. The pictures in television, in a certain way, correspond to the shared context of conversation and the resulting lack of elaboration, linguistically realized through the use of ellipsis, contractions, etc.

Scripted language has been studied as a representation of face-to-face conversation. Rey (2001), for example, used the American television show *Star Trek* for a diachronic and synchronic study of language and gender. In addition to stating that the popular media is an appropriate source for the study of sociolinguistic differences through the analysis of the speech of males and females, Rey points out that "while the language used in television is obviously not the same as unscripted language, it does represent the language scriptwriters imagine that real women and men produce" (p. 138).

On the nature of sitcoms, Bernan (1987) comments that

> the sitcom, which has displaced most other forms of video comedy, is supposed to "relate" to its audience. It does so in a number of ways, first by creating characters who are supposed to resemble and to represent the audience. Second, it dramatizes

events or conditions (for example the conflict of female liberation with male chauvinism) that provide motivation for a plot. Third, the sitcom suggests an attitude toward things, and toward ourselves. (p. 13)

Even though this was meant as a criticism on the lack of literary value of sitcoms, it suggests that the social relevance that seems to be a priority for the nature of sitcoms is likely to be expressed in a language that also resembles that of its audience. However, again, nothing is said about the linguistic realization of this 'language.'

Kaye and Sapolsky (2001) analyze the use of offensive language in prime-time television, but the authors limit their investigation to the amount of offensive language (a list of lexical items) in some shows, comparing its frequency between 1990 and 1997. Despite the recognized influence of the spoken media on processes of language change (e.g., Fitzmaurice, 2000) and the influence of the televised media on language use (Adams, 2000, on the frequency in which some of the nonstandard language used in the shows *Buffy the Vampire Slayer* and *The Simpsons* has been adopted by many fans of the shows), there seems to be a dearth of studies on the language of television from a linguistic point of view.

1.5 Why study the language of *Friends*?

The popularity of *Friends* has affected the American public in various ways, from the style of women's hairdos to the use of language. For example, the US-based web site *Crazyfads.com* (http://www.crazyfads.com/90s.htm) lists popular fads of the 1920s through 2000s. Among the fads of the 1990s are popular toys/games such as Pokémon, Beanie Babies, and Tickle Me Elmo, Napster (the online music-sharing service), and *Rachel's hairstyle*: "Many women in the 1990's start[ed] cutting their hair in the same hair style as Jennifer Aniston's character 'Rachel' on the popular television sitcom Friends." The UK-based online women's lifestyle magazine *FemaleFirst.co.uk* (http://www.femalefirst.co.uk/fashion/1782004.htm) goes further to say that Rachel's haircut "has been named as the most influential hairstyle of all time," adding that "the stunning actress made the layered bob famous in the mid-nineties when she played Rachel Green in the hit sitcom 'Friends', sparking millions of imitations around the world." [Retrieved July 19, 2006].

In terms of language, the use of the adverbial intensifier *so* modifying an adjective split by the negator *not* (as in *That is so not true*) or followed by a clause (as in *That is so not what this is!*), often used by the characters, has become a regular feature of American English conversation, not only among younger groups. At the pedagogical level, the recent interest in bringing natural conversation to the ESL (English as a Second Language) classroom along with the dearth of readily available spoken corpora and the difficulty in collecting spoken data have led some scholars to recommend the use of sitcoms in the ESL classroom, especially for pragmatic language teaching and learning (e.g., Washburn, 2001). Excerpts from *Friends* have been used (and are still being used) to exemplify features of conversational English in ESL classrooms in the United States.

Humor is not the sole responsible reason for the success of any comedy. Social analysts point out that situation comedies have always reflected numerous aspects of American culture, from the feminism of the 1970s to today's focus on personal choices. Winzenburg (2004) states that "sitcoms are the most popular type of programming on the most influential medium in history and have had a major impact on how we think and what we think about" (p. 11), adding that viewers "often associat[e] a particular show with a specific time of their life that emotionally meant something to them" (p. 11). As such, viewer identification no doubt plays a major goal in the success of a sitcom. And it is through *language* that this identification is achieved and popular culture is expressed and reflected. In addition to the popularity factor, the nature of *Friends* – a show about people who just sit around and talk – makes this sitcom an interesting object of study for linguistic analysis, both as a comparison to natural conversation and as an object of study in itself. Further, though beyond the scope of the present study, a show that spans over a period of ten years provides unique data for studies of language change in progress.

1.6 Summary

Awareness of how information, feelings, attitudes, and opinions are linguistically realized is essential for the understanding of conversation. The grammatical choices that speakers make are functionally motivated. I have shown that the use of hedges (e.g., *kind of*), for example, can be instrumental in reducing the impact that an overly direct statement can have. By the same token, the choice of adverbial intensifiers (e.g., *so*) may reflect the emotional nature of the exchanges. In short, different linguistic features reflect and are associated with the various discourse circumstances of conversation.

Despite the many different approaches used to study conversation, comprehensive grammatically-oriented analyses are rare. Television dialogue is a virtually unexplored research area. As Rey (2001) suggests, scripted language can arguably be an effective indicator of how natural conversation is perceived. There seems to be an agreement among scholars that, despite the natural restrictions imposed by the televised medium, television dialogue should *sound* natural; otherwise, viewer identification with the show characters can be negatively impacted, thus, potentially, affecting the success of the show.

The popularity and nature of *Friends* make this show an interesting object of study. In the present study, I compare *Friends* to natural conversation from a grammatical perspective. I include a large number of linguistic features associated with natural conversation in this comparison and provide numerous examples from both corpora. Ultimately, this is a descriptive, two-pronged investigation: even though the primary goal of the analysis is to provide a linguistic account of television dialogue, as portrayed in *Friends*, I also provide a comprehensive description of numerous linguistic features that typify conversation. I want to emphasize that, obviously, the results of this study should not be (and are not meant to be) generalized to television dialogue overall; even though they are limited to a particular genre (situation comedy) and to a particular show (*Friends*), I believe the study gives us a glimpse of the basic characteristics of television dialogue in American situation comedies and hope it will encourage other researchers to delve into this unexplored, yet exciting area of enquiry.

1.7 Overview of the book

Chapter 2, *Setting the stage: The main characters*, provides a description of the show, its main characters, and how the *friends* relate to one another. Much of this description is presented through numerous dialogue excerpts, thus not only introducing the characters to those unfamiliar with the show but also inviting readers to start analyzing the language of the show.

The methodology used in the present study is the focus of Chapter 3, *Behind the scenes: Methodology and data*. The two corpora are amply described quantitatively (number of files and words) and qualitatively (interaction types and topics). Topics such as corpus collection, data coding, concordancing, norming, and statistical significance are addressed. Chapter 4, *Take 1: Dimensions and similarities*, provides a brief description of multidimensional analysis (Biber, 1988) and presents the results of the multidimensional analysis of *Friends*, revealing that *Friends* shares the core linguistic features that characterize natural conversation.

Unlike Chapter 4, Chapters 5 through 8 are essentially about functional differences between the two corpora. Chapter 5, *Some you know I mean it's really urgh: Vague language*, focuses on the 'vague devices' commonly used in conversation related to reasons that range from the undesirable impact of overly direct utterances to lexical gap to the pressures of real-time production. The expression of emotion is the topic of Chapter 6, *I am just really really happy...: Emotional language*. This analysis shows how the tone of verbal exchanges can be perceived based on the speakers' grammatical choices, even without information on intonation, volume of voice, and nonverbal clues (e.g., gestures, facial expression). Informal language is covered in Chapter 7, *I'm just hanging out. Y'know, having fun*: *Informal language*. The linguistic expression of informality is explored here through the analysis of features such as slang, expletives, and syntactic innovations.

Chapter 8, *Once upon a time: Narrative language*, addresses the multifaceted nature of registers. Acknowledging the importance of studying registers from a multidimensional perspective, this chapter focuses on the different degrees of narrativeness found in *Friends* and naturally-occurring conversation, discussing the distinction between narrative discourse and discourse immediacy. Chapter 9, *That's a wrap: Implications and applications*, concludes the book with a summary of the findings of the study, research applications, pedagogical implications, and suggestions for future research.

Setting the stage

The main characters

2.1 The show

The US situation comedy *Friends* premiered in the fall of 1994. During the show's ten-year run, it received a staggering number of awards and nominations and was considered the most popular television show in the United States and around the world in the last decade. A simple search in *Google* will retrieve dozens of hits, including numerous fan clubs all over the world, even after the show was discontinued. Video cassettes, DVDs, posters of the show and of individual actors, and trivia games are some of the many commercially available products carrying the *Friends* trademark.

The show portrays a group of six twenty-something friends living in New York City. The *friends* find comfort and support in one another as they struggle to achieve professional success and find happiness. Friendship, relationships, love, and sex are constant themes in this series. Humor is created against a backdrop of social and moral issues that pervaded the 1990s and continue to be controversial in the 2000s. Among these issues is same-sex marriage, artificial insemination, surrogate mothers, and age difference in romantic relationships. In addition, the show captures personal concerns shared by a large number of viewers ranging from family issues to career goals to the fear of 'ending up alone'. In other words, humor is not created in a social vacuum; the situations lived by the characters reflect a facet of American culture, and this real-life aspect of the show may have contributed to its immense popularity.

2.2 The main characters

Most interactions revolve around the six main characters of the show: Monica (Courteney Cox), Rachel (Jennifer Aniston), Phoebe (Lisa Kudrow), Ross (David Schwimmer), Chandler (Matthew Perry), and Joey (Matt Le Blanc). Monica, Ross (Monica's older brother), and Rachel have been friends since their high school years; Chandler and Ross met in college and have been close friends ever since;

Phoebe used to be Monica's roommate but moved out to live with her grandmother because she could not stand Monica's obsession with cleanliness and order; Joey joined the group of friends when he became Cha ndler's roommate and the two of them have been best friends ever since. All of this precedes the beginning of the show. The audience becomes privy to some of these details in a special flashback episode in season 3 (*The One With the Flashback*).

2.2.1 The individual characters

Information on the characters, plot, episode guides, and transcripts can be found in several online fan clubs – all with a remarkable attention to detail[1]. Next, I provide a brief account of the characters, how they relate to one another, and a few excerpts of the show. This description is not intended to be a profound analysis of social ties or individual psychological profiles; rather, it is meant to provide those unfamiliar with the show with an overall picture of the relationships shared by the characters, which, ultimately, lay the groundwork for the types of topics addressed in the show and the language utilized by the characters.

a. *Monica* (34 years old[2] at the end of the series): She is Ross's sister, used to be overweight in high school and was often teased by her classmates and friends. She still has a difficult relationship with her mother, who always finds fault in what she does. Throughout the show she works as a cook, a head chef, and has her own catering business for a brief period of time. She is an obsessive cleaner, excessively competitive, and is considered bossy and controlling by her own friends. She shares an apartment with Rachel for most of the series. After several unsuccessful romantic relationships (with men outside of the group of *friends*), Monica starts dating Chandler in season 5, starts living with him in season 6, and ends up marrying him in season 7. In the last season, the couple fulfill their dream of starting a family by adopting two children.

---

1.   For more detailed information on the show, characters, and plot see, for example: http://www.friends-tv.org/epguide.html; http://www.geocities.com/friends_greatestsitcom/about.htm; and http://livesinabox.com/friends/.

2.   All of the characters' ages are based on clues given in several episodes throughout the ten seasons. In season 3, Monica stated that she was "25 and 13 months," which makes her 34 in the last season. I included the age of the characters because it may provide insight into generation-related issues, which are likely to affect the production of language. In addition, the fact that the show comprises spoken data spanning over a period of ten years points to the uniqueness of the data as they are likely to capture processes of language change in progress.

Excerpt 1: In season 4, episode 13 (*The One With Rachel's Crush*), Phoebe agrees to be the surrogate mother for her brother, Frank, Jr. and his wife, Alice. In this excerpt, she refers to Monica's obesity in high school.

Phoebe: Oh, hey, Mon, do you still have your like... old blouses and dresses from high school?

Monica: Yeah, I think I have some around here somewhere. Why?

Phoebe: Well, it's just that maternity clothes are so expensive...

Excerpt 2: This dialogue exemplifies the difficult relationship Monica has with her mother (Mrs. Geller). In season 4, episode 3 (*The One With The Cuffs*), Monica's mother hires her to cater a party for her. Monica discovers she lost a nail in one of the dishes she was cooking and, as she tells her mother the bad news, she learns that her mother had bet on her failure.

Monica: Okay ah, please don't freak out. Umm, but ah, there's a blue fingernail in one of the quiche cups, and there's no way to know which one...

Phoebe: And! Whoever finds it wins the prize!

Mrs. Geller: (laughs) I'm not freaking out.

Monica: Then why are you laughing?

Mrs. Geller: It's nothing; it's just that now your Father owes me five dollars.

Monica: What? You bet I'd lose a nail?

Mrs. Geller: Oh no, don't be silly. I just bet I'd need these. (Opens the freezer to reveal...)

Monica: Frozen lasagnas?

Mrs. Geller: Um-hmm.

Monica: You bet that I'd screw up?! So all that stuff about hiring me because I was good was...

Mrs. Geller: No-no-no, that was all true. This was just in case you *pulled a Monica*.

Monica: You promised Dr. Weinburg, you'd never use that phrase.

Excerpt 3: Monica is playing ping pong with Chandler (already married to Monica), Phoebe, and Mike (who marries Phoebe in the last season) in season 9, episode 24 (*The One In Barbados, part 2*). The dialogue shows Monica's exacerbated competitiveness and makes reference to her cleaning obsession.

(Chandler and Phoebe look bored to death. Monica scores and laughs)

Mike: Ok, so it's a tie again, 41 to 41.

Chandler: (exhausted) Ok, look! Enough is enough!

Monica: No, I have just to have two more points to beat him!

Chandler:	Monica, that was also true an hour ago! I mean, please, look at you! Your hand is blistered you can barely stand, your hair is inexplicable! Ok, you've already proven you are just as good as he is, now we've missed our dinner reservations, so now let's just go upstairs, order room service, take a shower and shave your head!
Monica:	I can't just walk away! I've put in four hours!
Chandler:	But...
Monica:	Look! You knew this about me when you married me! You agreed to take me in sickness and in health. Well, this is my sickness!
Chandler:	What about the obsessive cleaning?
Monica:	That's just good sense!

b. *Rachel* (35 years old at the end of the series): Monica's best friend in high school, Rachel is a spoiled girl who lived off her father's money until the beginning of the show. She becomes Monica's roommate in the first episode of the first season after having left her fiancé at the altar. Having never held a job before, she works as a waitress at *Central Perk* (a coffee house where the *friends* often 'hang out'), at *Bloomingdale's* as an assistant buyer, and then at *Ralph Lauren* as the women's collection coordinator. Rachel finds out that Ross has had 'a crush' on her since 9th grade and starts dating him in season 2. The couple break up in season 3, get drunk in season 5 in Las Vegas and end up getting married. Realizing it had been a mistake, they divorce in the following season. Also in season 6, Rachel shares an apartment with Phoebe and then with Joey.

Because of a 'one-night stand', she has a daughter with Ross in season 8 and moves in with him so he can also take care of the baby in spite of no longer being romantically involved with him. She and Ross end up together in the end of the series.

> Excerpt 4: In the first episode of season 1 (*The One Where Monica Gets A Roommate*), Rachel leaves her fiancé at the altar and goes to look for Monica at *Central Perk*. There, still wearing her wedding dress, she calls her father to explain her unexpected decision. The dialogue reveals her financial dependence on her father.
>
> | Rachel: | Look Daddy, it's my life. Well maybe I'll just stay here with Monica. |
> |---|---|
> | Monica: | Well, I guess we've established who's staying here with Monica... |
> | Rachel: | Well, maybe that's my decision. Well, maybe I don't need your money. Wait!! Wait, I said maybe!! |

<u>Excerpt 5</u>: Rachel is perceived as a "spoiled daddy's girl" even by Mr. Treeger, the apartment building maintenance person. In this segment (season 4, episode 4, *The One With The Ballroom Dancing*), Rachel takes the trash out to the trash chute (for the first time) and tries to push down a large box of pizza (which still has two slices of pizza in it), but the box is too big and gets stuck. The following dialogue with Mr. Treeger ensues:

Mr. Treeger: What are you doing?

Rachel: Ummm. Oh! I'm sorry. (She grabs the box of pizza and offers him a piece.) It's a little old but…

Mr. Treeger: No! You're clogging up the chute that I spent a half-hour un-clogging!

Rachel: I'm sorry. I didn't—I don't come in here a lot.

Mr. Treeger: 'Cause you're a little princess! "Daddy, buy me a pizza. Daddy, buy me a candy factory. Daddy, make the cast of *Cats* sing Happy Birthday to me…"

Rachel: I didn't… I never said that.

Mr. Treeger: You think you could make a mess and the big man in coveralls will come in here and clean it up, huh? Well, why don't you think of someone else for a change?

Rachel: (starting to cry) Okay, I'm sorry. (Runs out still carrying the pizza box.)

c. Phoebe (34 or 35 years old at the end of the series): Of all of the characters, Phoebe has the most complicated family relationships: she left home when she was 14, after her mother committed suicide (and her "stepfather was back in jail"); she has a twin sister, Ursula, whom she rarely sees and with whom she has a bad relationship; in season 3, she finds out she has a brother, Frank, Jr., and she finally meets her father in her grandmother's memorial service in season 5. In the special "flashback episode" (season 3), the audience learns she used to share an apartment with Monica, but left to live with her grandmother. Phoebe works as a masseuse for some time and often sings her 'weird songs' (many of which are about death) at *Central Perk*. In season 4, she agrees to be the surrogate mother for her brother and much older wife, Alice. Described in one of the many *Friends'* online fan clubs[3] as "way out in left field most of the time," Phoebe believes she can cleanse auras and feel the presence of dead people; her 'spacey' and very funny character often creates humor with unexpected comments and reactions. In season 9, she gets seriously involved with Mike (not one of the *friends*) whom she marries in the last season.

---

3.   Friends, Greatest Sitcom: http://geocities.com/friends_greatestsitcom/.

Excerpt 6: In this segment (season 1, episode 1, *The One Where Monica Gets A Roommate*), the *friends* are trying to convince Rachel to cut up her credit cards, so she can stop depending on her father and start living her own life. Phoebe intervenes and reminds the group of how hard it is to start living on one's own.

Monica: C'mon, you can't live off your parents your whole life.

Rachel: I know that. That's why I was getting married.

Phoebe: Give her a break, it's hard being on your own for the first time.

Rachel: Thank you.

Phoebe: You're welcome. I remember when I first came to this city. I was fourteen. My mom had just killed herself and my step-dad was back in prison, and I got here, and I didn't know anybody. And I ended up living with this albino guy who was, like, cleaning windshields outside port authority, and then he killed himself, and then I found aromatherapy. So believe me, I know exactly how you feel.

Excerpt 7: In the same episode (season 1, episode 1), as Ross is telling the *friends* about how he feels about his ex-wife leaving him, Phoebe attempts to use her 'spiritual powers.'

Monica: (to Ross) Let me get you some coffee.

Ross: Thanks.

Phoebe: Ooh! Oh! (She starts to pluck at the air just in front of Ross.)

Ross: No, no don't! Stop cleansing my aura! No, just leave my aura alone, okay?

Phoebe: Fine! Be murky!

Excerpt 8: This segment shows one of Phoebe's unexpected comments. In season 1, episode 10 (*The One With The Monkey*), Ross brings a monkey home (Marcel). Phoebe asks Ross where he had gotten the monkey and offers the following reaction to Ross's answer:

Ross: Guys? There's a somebody I'd like you to meet. (A monkey jumps on to his shoulder.)

All: Oooh!

Monica: W-wait. What is that?

Ross: 'That' would be Marcel. You wanna say hi?

Monica: No, no, I don't.

Rachel: Oh, he is precious! Where did you get him?

Ross: My friend Bethel rescued him from some lab.

Phoebe: That is so cruel! Why? Why would a parent name their child Bethel?

d. Ross (35 years old at the end of the series): The most well-educated of the characters, Ross (Monica's brother), a paleontologist, goes through difficult relationship problems: he has a son, Ben, with his ex-wife, Carol, who leaves him for another woman in season 1 after she discovers she is a lesbian; having had a 'crush' on Rachel since 9th grade, Ross starts dating her in season 2, but the couple break up in season 3; at the end of season 4/beginning of season 5 he marries Rachel's boss' niece Emily, but accidentally calls Emily "Rachel" as he says his vows at the altar. They proceed with the ceremony, but the relationship does not work. In season 8, after a one-night stand, he has a daughter with Rachel. Ross and Rachel end up together in the last season of the series. Ross lives by himself for most of the show, but spends most of his free time with the *friends* at Monica and Rachel's apartment or at *Central Perk*.

> Excerpt 9: In the opening scene of the show, Ross tells everyone how he feels about his ex-wife's leaving him for another woman:
> Monica: Are you okay, sweetie?
> Ross: I just feel like someone reached down my throat, grabbed my small intestine, pulled it out of my mouth and tied it around my neck...

> Excerpt 10: In the second episode of season 1 (*The One With The Sonogram At The End*), Ross explains to his parents the reason for his divorce, which will haunt him throughout the series.
> Monica: So, Ross, what's going on with you? Any stories? (Digs her elbow into his hand.) No news, no little anecdotes to share with the folks?
> Ross: Okay! Okay. (To his parents) Look, I, uh I realize you guys have been wondering what exactly happened between Carol and me, and, so, well, here's the deal. Carol's a lesbian. She's living with a woman named Susan. She's pregnant with my child, and she and Susan are going to raise the baby.

> Excerpt 11: In season 3, episode 23 (*The One With Ross's Thing*), a misunderstanding leads the *friends* to believe that Pete, Monica's boyfriend at the time, is planning to propose to her. When Ross expresses his opinion about the hasty decision, Rachel brings up his marriage to a lesbian.
> Monica: Would you stop? We've only been going out a couple of weeks, I mean we don't even know if he's gonna propose.

Chandler:	Yes, but this is Pete. Okay? He's not like other people, on your first date he took you to Rome. For most guys that's like a third or fourth date kinda thing.
Monica:	Well if-if that's what it is, then it's-it's crazy.
Ross:	Monica's right. We're talking about getting married here. Okay? She-she can't just rush into this.
Rachel:	Oh please, what do you know! You married a lesbian!

<u>Excerpt 12</u>: In season 4, episode 18 (*The One With Rachel's New Dress*), Ross's ex-wife's lover, Susan, goes to London on a business trip and arranges to spend time with Ross's fiancée at the time, Emily. In this segment, he shows his paranoid concern in a dialogue with his ex-wife, Carol:

Ross:	So umm, any word from Susan?
Carol:	Oh, yeah! She said she's having *so* much fun with Emily.
Ross:	Uh-huh. Uh-huh. Uh, by the by, did it uh, did it ever occur to you that, I don't know, maybe they might be having a little too much fun?
Carol:	What's *too* much fun?
Ross:	Y'know, the kind of fun, you and Susan had when we were married.
Carol:	Oh my God, you are so paranoid!
Ross:	Am I?!
Carol:	Yes!
Ross:	Am I?!
Carol:	I can't speak for Emily, but Susan is in a loving, committed relationship.
Ross:	Uh-huh, Carol, so were we. All right, just-just imagine for a moment, Susan meets someone and-and they really hit it off. Y'know? Say-say they're coming back from the theater, and they-they stop at a pub for a couple of drinks, they're laughing, y'know, someone innocently touches someone else… There's electricity, it's new. It's exciting. Are you telling me there isn't even the slightest possibility of something happening?
Carol:	Maybe.
Ross:	OH MY GOD!! I didn't really believe it until you just said it!!

e. Chandler (35 years old at the end of the series): Afraid of romantic commitments, Chandler is insecure with women; he has difficulty asking them out as well as breaking up with them. He is said to use humor "as a defense mechanism" and often makes self-deprecating comments. After some unsuccessful relationships, he starts dating Monica in season 5, moves in with her in season 6, and marries her in season 7. The couple adopt two babies in the last season. Chandler and Joey share an apartment for most of the series and also 'hang out' at Monica and Rachel's apartment or at *Central Perk* with the other friends most of the time. Probably the funniest of all characters, he became famous for his witty one-liners: "Sometimes I wish I was a lesbian – did I say that out loud?" He works in a data-processing company, but nobody knows exactly what he does.

> Excerpt 13: In the first episode of season 1, Monica is trying to convince everyone that she is not really going out on a *date*. In a self-deprecating comment, Chandler provides a picture of his difficulty in relating to women:
>
> Monica: Okay, everybody relax. This is not even a date. It's just two people going out to dinner and not having sex.
> Chandler: Sounds like a date to me.
>
> Excerpt 14: In season 2, episode 13 (*The One After The Superbowl, part 2*), Chandler himself alludes to his use of humor as a "defense mechanism."
>
> Susie: It's nice to see you're not still wearing that denim cap with all the little mirrors on it.
> Chandler: Oh, right, well yeah, I graduated fourth grade and realized I wasn't a pimp.
> Susie: Remember the class play? You, you pulled up my skirt and the entire auditorium saw my underpants.
> Chandler: Yes, back then I, uh, used humor as a defense mechanism. Thank God I don't do that anymore.
>
> Excerpt 15: In season 1, episode 15 (*The One With The Stoned Guy*), Chandler offers one of his many witty one-liners as Monica describes what she believes is a perfect restaurant for her purposes:
>
> Monica: Steve's restaurant is not too big, not too small, just right!
> Chandler: Was it formerly owned by a blonde woman and some bears?

f. Joey (36 years old at the end of the last season): Joey is a laidback womanizer who never had a lasting relationship. An aspiring actor, he lands several unimportant roles until he reaches the 'highlight' of his acting career: a short-lived role as Dr. Drake Ramorey in *Days of Our lives*[4]. The real 'break' in his career, though, *would have been* a role in a movie with Al Pacino as Al Pacino's "butt double," but he tries too hard to 'act' the part and gets fired. Portrayed as not very bright intellectually, he delivers some of the funniest lines in the show, which reveal this personal trait.

---

4.   *Days of Our Lives* is a popular day-time soap opera in the United States.

Joey meets the other *friends* (except Rachel whom he meets in the first episode of the first season) before the show begins when he becomes Chandler's roommate. The three excerpts below illustrate Joey's less than bright intellect:

> Excerpt 16: Joey and Chandler are 'hanging out' at *Central Perk*. Chandler is reading the newspaper.
> Joey: Can I see the comics?
> Chandler: This is the *New York Times*!
> Joey: Okay… *MAY* I see the comics?

> Excerpt 17: In the tenth episode of season 4 (*The One With The Girl From Poughkeepsie*), Monica gets a job as head chef in a restaurant she had written a scathing review about and has trouble being respected by her subordinates. Chandler comes up with an idea, and Joey offers to help.
> Chandler: Hey, you know what you can do? I remember reading about this director, I think it was Orson Wells, who at the beginning of the movie would hire somebody, just so he could fire them in front of everybody. Then they would all know who's boss.
> Joey: Hey, Mon! I'm not doing anything, why don't you fire me?
> Monica: That's a good idea! Wait, do you know how to waiter?
> Joey: Good enough to get fired.
> Monica: All right, you're hired!
> Joey: Hey! That must be why I got fired last week! Does this Orson Wells guy direct Burger King commercials?
> Chandler: (he glares at him for a while in disbelief) Yes…

> Excerpt 18: In this segment, knowing that Joey is dating two women, Chandler (who is interested in one of them) tries to convince Joey that he should make a decision, choose one of the women, and settle down…
> Chandler: All right look, I think it's time for you to settle down. Y'know? Make a choice, pick a lane.
> Joey: Who's Elaine?

2.3 Summary

In this chapter, the overall nature of *Friends* and the relationships shared by the characters were described. In addition, a summary of the major personal traits of each of the characters was provided and several excerpts of the show were used to exemplify some of these traits. I hope to have provided enough information to those unfamiliar with the show. I believe this overview of the show and the characters is important because the closeness of relationships directly influences the way speakers make grammatical and lexical choices to convey informality, formality, stance, opinions, and feelings. Keeping this information in mind makes it easier to notice that oftentimes humor is created through pragmatic failure or unexpected responses and reactions. The way in which the addition of humor may negatively impact the naturalness of the dialogues in *Friends* is addressed throughout the book.

CHAPTER 3

Behind the scenes
Methodology and data

3.1 Introduction

In the present study, I take a corpus-based/grammatical approach to compare the scripted language of *Friends* to natural conversation. I combine multidimensional methodology (Biber, 1988) with a frequency-based analysis of a large number of linguistic features associated with the typical characteristics of face-to-face conversation. In this chapter, I focus on the description of the two corpora, including an analysis of the most typical types of interactions and topics found in them. I also explain how the data were coded, how searches were conducted, and briefly address the issues of norming and statistical significance. In the last section of the chapter, I introduce the notion of functional differences, which provides the framework for the analysis of the topics discussed in Chapters 5 through 8. Multidimensional analysis (Biber, 1988) was used in the first part of the present study and is thus an integral part of the methodology. For ease of reference, I introduce this methodology along with the results of the multidimensional analysis of *Friends* in Chapter 4.

3.2 The data

In addition to corpus size and design, several factors must be considered in corpus-based analysis of spoken language. Among these factors are speaker attributes (e.g., age, sex), settings (e.g., at home, business office), and types of interactions[1] (e.g., casual conversation, service encounter). As Biber and Conrad (2001) point out, corpus-based analysis is much more than *bean counting*. Initial frequency counts can point to important differences (or similarities) in the comparison of corpora; however, it is the interaction of all of these situational factors that allows for the functional interpretation of the data.

In the next sections, the American television show corpus (referred to as the *Friends* corpus) and the American English conversation corpus are described.

---

1. Types of interactions are often referred to as speech types in the literature.

First, I explain how the *Friends* corpus was collected and provide a snapshot of the most common settings and types of interactions identified in the corpus. The corpus of American English conversation is then described, including an account of the most frequent settings and types of interactions along with the rationale for the selection of texts used for comparisons with the *Friends* corpus.

3.2.1 The *Friends* corpus: Composition

The *Friends* corpus comprises *transcripts* (not scripts) of nine seasons of the show (from 1994 to 2003) and has approximately 600,000 words. The show episodes were transcribed (after the shows were aired) by several online fan clubs. The data used for analysis was taken from one of these fan clubs, *Crazy for Friends* (http://www.livesinabox.com/friends/). This fan club made free transcripts of the show available for educational and entertainment purposes. This particular fan club was chosen because of the quality of the transcriptions. Transcripts of three episodes from each season (a total of 27 episodes) were randomly selected and compared with the actual videos of the shows. The transcripts were not only fairly accurate but also extremely detailed, including several features that scripts are not likely to present: hesitators (e.g., *um, er, uh*), pauses (e.g., –; *[pause]*), repeats (e.g., *it's it's it's*), contractions (e.g., *you're*), and even descriptions of the scenes and actors' performances (e.g., *looks sadly at Ross; struggling to concentrate*).

Each episode of the show was copied from the fan club web site and saved as a text file identifying the season and the episode (e.g., file 519 indicates that it contains the nineteenth episode of the fifth season). Table 3–1 shows the composition of the *Friends* corpus.

Table 3.1 Composition of the *Friends* corpus

Seasons	# of episodes	# of words	Average # of words/episode
1 (1994–1995)	24	60,180	2,507
2 (1995–1996)	23	65,364	2,842
3 (1996–1997)	25	67,994	2,720
4 (1997–1998)	23	71,732	3,119
5 (1998–1999)	24	57,460	2,394
6 (1999–2000)	23	69,652	3,028
7 (2000–2001)	23	60,882	2,647
8 (2001–2002)	23	76,205	3,313
9 (2002–2003)	24	75,298	3,137
Total	206	604,767	2,935

As mentioned earlier, the *Friends* transcripts contained descriptions of scenes and actors' performances. One version of the corpus was saved with this contextual information because scene descriptions can be very important for the comprehension of dialogues that are extremely context-dependent. However, for frequency counts and the analysis of grammatical features, a second version of the corpus was created without these descriptions. A simple computer program was written to remove these comments (which were always provided in square brackets or parentheses).

3.2.2   The *Friends* corpus: Settings and interactions

The version of the *Friends* corpus containing contextual information (i.e., description of scenes and actors' performances) was useful not only for the comprehension of more content-dependent dialogues but also for the identification of the major settings and types of interactions characterizing the television show. This sampling of settings and types of interactions was carried out with the analysis of every fifth episode of each of the nine seasons (approximately 41 episodes). This process was facilitated by the description of the scenes contained in this version of the corpus. Once the beginning of each scene was found, the dialogues were read, and the type of interactions or overall topic was identified. Below is an example of the result of one of these searches, showing the scene description and part of the dialogue that followed it.

[Scene: Chandler and Joey's, Joey is reading the paper and Chandler is getting ready for work.]

Rachel:	(entering) Hey! Umm, do you guys have any juice?
Joey:	Just pickle.
Chandler:	Hey uh, Rach, funny story. I ah, bumped into Joanna on the street yesterday.
Rachel:	My boss, Joanna? Wow, that must've been awkward.
Chandler:	Well, no, actually she uh, asked me if I wanted to get a drink.
Rachel:	(laughs) You ah, you didn't say 'Yes' to that did you?
Chandler:	(laughs) No. No!
Joanna:	(Coming out of the shower wearing nothing but a towel) Hello, Rachel. (She goes into Chandler's bedroom)
Chandler:	Well, not at first.

[*Friends*: Season 4, episode 3, *The One With The Cuffs*]

Table 3.2 Summary of settings and types of interactions in *Friends*

Settings	Types of interactions
Central Perk	Discussing things only guys can do (e.g., pee standing up) and only women can do (e.g., take out bra without taking off blouse)
Central Perk	Discussing date plans for Saturday night
Monica and Rachel's apartment	Joey is trying to convince Monica to pose as his girlfriend
A fancy restaurant	A blind date situation
At a Laundromat	Ross is showing Rachel how to do laundry… 'hitting on' her
The ladies' room at a restaurant	Monica and Angela are 'talking about guys'
Central Perk	Phoebe is coaching Chandler on how to break up with Janice
Central Perk	Discussing plans for New Year's and how bad it is not to have a 'partner' in this occasion
Chandler's office	Chandler interacts with supervisor
Monica's apartment	Making food
Chandler and Joey's	Discussing how Ross's date the previous night did not end up with sex
Monica and Rachel's	Monica is trying to convince Rachel to waitress for her
Monica and Rachel's	Monica and Phoebe are preparing for a barbecue for Rachel's birthday and talking about Joey's steady date
Central Perk	Talking about how to quit smoking
Central Perk	Playing the keyboard / friends listen and make comments
At the beach	Playing games; talking about sex partners; dating

Table 3.2 shows a summary of the most frequent scenes and types of interactions identified in the *Friends* corpus. *Central Perk*, a coffee house, is listed six times because this is the place where the group of friends meets regularly. Several of the episodes begin and end at *Central Perk*. The apartments where the characters live are another very frequent setting. In spite of the fact that these are by far the most frequent settings in the show, there are also scenes in other places such as in restaurants, in the street, or in offices where one or two of the characters work.

This first analysis reveals not only a limited number of settings (as compared to the conversation corpus; see Section 3.2.5) in which the characters' interactions take place, but also an extremely restricted range of conversation topics, which typically involve relationships, dating, and sex. In Excerpt # 1, the characters start talking about their plans for New Year's. The topic of the conversation then shifts to relationships and how hard it is not to have a partner in such an occasion. In Excerpt # 2, even though the purpose of being together at Monica and Rachel's apartment was to prepare a barbecue for Rachel's birthday, the conversation quickly moves to Joey's current relationship.

Excerpt # 1:

Rachel: Hey, do you guys know what you're doing for New Year's? (They all protest and hit her with cushions) Gee, what?! What is wrong with New Year's?

Chandler: Nothing for you, you have Paolo. You don't have to face the horrible pressures of this holiday: desperate scramble to find anything with lips just so you can have someone to kiss when the ball drops!! Man, I'm talking loud!

Rachel: Well, for your information, Paolo is gonna be in Rome this New Year, so I'll be just as pathetic as the rest of you.

Phoebe: Yeah, you wish!

Chandler: It's just that I'm sick of being a victim of this Dick Clark holiday. I say this year, no dates, we make a pact. Just the six of us-dinner.

All: Yeah, okay. Alright.

Chandler: Y'know, I was hoping for a little more enthusiasm.

All: Woooo! Yeah!

[*Friends*: Season 1, episode 10, *The One With the Monkey*]

Excerpt # 2:

Monica: Oh Joey, Melanie called, said she's gonna be late.

Joey: Oh, OK.

Phoebe: So how are things going with you two? Is she becoming your (provocatively) special someone?

Joey: I don't know, she's, uh.... she's pretty great.

Monica: Yeah? What does she think of your little science project?

Joey: What, you think I'm gonna tell a girl I like that I'm also seeing a cup?

Monica: Man's got a point.

Joey: Well, the tough thing is, she really wants to have sex with me.

Chandler: Crazy bitch.

[*Friends*: Season 1, episode 24, *The One Where Rachel Finds Out*]

Perhaps the second most striking characteristic of the dialogues in *Friends* is their frequent reference to immediate problems or events that have taken place recently or that are going on at the time of the interaction. Unlike what often occurs in narrative chunks of naturally-occurring conversation, the turn structure tends to be evenly distributed in *Friends*. Excerpts # 3 and # 4 illustrate what I call *discourse immediacy* (see Chapter 8, Section 8.4) that characterizes many of the dialogues in the show.

> *Excerpt # 3:*
> Joey: What a tool!
> Rachel: You don't want to work for a guy like that.
> Ross: Yeah!
> Monica: I know... it's just... I thought this was, you know... it.
> Ross: Look, you'll get there. You're an amazing chef.
> Phoebe: Yeah! You know all those yummy noises? I wasn't faking.
> [*Friends*: Season 1, episode 15, *The One With The Stoned Guy*]
>
> *Excerpt # 4:*
> Chandler: I haven't... I haven't even thought about the results yet... I just assumed that everything was gonna be ok.
> Janice: Oh! Well, you know what? It probably is.
> Chandler: Yeah, but what if it's not? What if there is a reason why we can't have a baby?
> Janice: Oh, Chandler, look. You and Monica are meant to have children. I am sure it's gonna be just fine.
> [*Friends*: Season 9, episode 21, *The One With The Fertility Test*]

The main characters of the show share very close relationships. They are either best friends, like Joey and Chandler, or have intimate relationships, like Ross and Rachel (who were lovers for some time), and Chandler and Monica (who got married in season 7). As a result of these close relationships, several interactions tend to involve the theme of friendship or relationships, and thus tend to be emotionally loaded. In Excerpt # 5, for example, Joey and Chandler had a heated argument over a woman they were both romantically interested in.

> *Excerpt # 5:*
> Chandler: Yeah, I mean when you were late last night, Kathy and I got to talking, and one thing led to another and...
> Joey: And what?! Did you sleep with her?!
> Chandler: No! No! No! I just kissed her.
> Joey: What?!! That's even worse!!
> Chandler: How is that worse?!
> Joey: I don't know! But it's the same!
> Chandler: Look, I'm sorry! But there's nothing I can do. I think I'm in love with her!

Joey:	Who cares?! You went behind my back! I would never do that to you!
Chandler:	You're right, I have no excuses! I was totally over the line.
Joey:	Over the line?! You-you're-you're so far past the line, that you-you can't even see the line! The line is a dot to you!
Chandler:	Yes. Yes! Right! And I feel horrible. You have to believe me!
Joey:	Is that why you bought all this stuff?! I (Chandler makes a face like "Well, kinda.") Well, y'know what? I will not watch your TV, I will not listen to your stereo, and there's a cinnamon raisin loaf in the new bread maker that I'm not gonna eat! You know why?!
Chandler:	Probably because…
Joey:	Because it's all tainted with your betrayal. From now on this apartment is empty for me! And I'm not happy about you either. (The bread maker dings) Oh, and just so you know, I made that bread for you. (Joey walks into his bedroom and slams the door.)

[*Friends*: Season 6, episode 20, *The One With Mac And C.H.E.E.S.E.*]

Finally, another characteristic of the show is the extremely frequent greeting exchanges. Several scenes (especially those at *Central Perk* and in Monica and Rachel's apartment) begin with one (or more) of the characters arriving and greeting the others, as in Excerpt # 6.

Excerpt # 6:
[Scene: Central Perk, the next day Rachel, Phoebe, and Chandler are there as Monica enters.]

Monica:	Hey guys!
Chandler:	Hey-hey.
Rachel:	Hi. Monica!
Monica:	Hey. (Sits down on the arm of the couch.)
Rachel:	Hi boots.

[Season 8, episode 10, *The One With Monica's Boots*]

To sum it up, the overall analysis of settings and interactions in *Friends* reveals a rather restricted range of settings and types of interactions with topics typically restricted to relationships, dating, and sex. The close relationships shared by the characters are reflected in the frequent emotionally loaded exchanges. The turns are typically evenly distributed due to the discourse immediacy that characterizes the dialogues. Finally, the extremely high frequency of greeting exchanges results from the structure of the scenes, which often start with the characters meeting one another.

3.2.3 The Conversation corpus: Composition

The American conversation subcorpus of the *Longman Grammar Corpus* has approximately 4,000,000 words. Carefully designed to be representative of American English conversation, it includes a wide range of settings (e.g. park, family home, classroom), types of interactions (e.g., casual conversations, task-related, telephone conversations), geographical regions (i.e., states, cities) and speaker attributes (e.g., age, sex, occupation, years of schooling). The informants who took part in the collection of this corpus tape-recorded all of their conversations over a period of a week. These recordings were then transcribed and saved electronically for linguistic research purposes. Each of the conversations (referred to as texts) includes headers, preceding the transcriptions, containing the information mentioned above (e.g., settings, types of interactions). A simplified version of these headers (with information about one of the speakers) is shown below for illustrative purposes.

<TAPE_#>	1092
<TAPE_TITLE>	Waiting for the Sheets
<DATE_RECORDED>	1-Sep-94
<STATE_RECORDED>	MI
<SETTING/ROOM>	motel room
<EVENT_TYPE>	face to face conversation
<EVENT>	waiting for another couple so we can go to breakfast
<SPEAKER_#>	944
<FIRST_NAME>	J. Peter
<AGE>	55
<SEX>	M
<NATIVE_LANGUAGE>	English
<NATIVE_DIALECT>	Bay City
<DIALECT_STATE>	MI
<CITY_CURRENT>	South Lyon
<STATE_CURRENT>	MI
<OCCUPATION>	Laser/robotics engineer
<HIGHEST_SCHOOLING>	Some college
<YEARS_OF_SCHOOLING>	13
<ETHNICITY>	White

For the purposes of the present study, a subcorpus of the American conversation corpus of approximately the same size as the *Friends* corpus (590,000 words) was created. This was done to make the searches for some of linguistic features more manageable. For the most part, frequency counts were done automatically. In some cases, however, every instance of a particular word (or grammatical feature) had to be checked manually for accuracy. For example, *totally* is analyzed as an adverbial intensifier (as in *I think it's totally insane…*) in Chapter 6 and is classified as a marker of emotionally-loaded language; in Chapter 7, it is described as syntactic innovation used with the meaning of emphatic agreement, as in

> Phoebe: He's holding us back.
> Ross: <u>Totally</u>.

In this context, *totally* is analyzed as a marker of informality. All of the instances of *totally* had to then be checked individually for accuracy.

3.2.4 The American conversation subcorpus

An initial analysis of the transcripts and their headers had revealed that some of the speakers were not identified in some the transcripts (possibly because of the difficulty the transcribers had in the precise identification of the voices) and/or some of the header information was incomplete. Knowing that this information (who said what to whom) could potentially be important for functional interpretations, one of the criteria for the selection of texts was the availability of speaker information; the other was the proportional representation of the major types of settings and interactions. To ascertain that these conditions be met, the following steps were taken:

– Based on the headers of the 716 texts comprising the American conversation portion of the *Longman Grammar Corpus*, a file containing the description of the settings, types of interactions, number of speakers, and age of the speakers of each text was created. Information on dialects, gender, and schooling was not included because analyses involving these data were beyond the scope of the present study;

– Only texts that had complete header information on the four fields (i.e., settings, types of interactions, number of speakers, and age of speakers) were selected;

– Of the remaining texts, those that consistently did not have speaker identification in the dialogues (indicated by <?>), as in file 055801 below, were eliminated. This was done because this information (who said what to whom) can also be crucial for functional interpretations of linguistic features.

<?> Did you manage?

<?> Yeah.

<?> Well, how, that's very clever of you. I've been trying to open one for <nv_laugh>.

<?> Do you have fingernails?

<?> Yeah you have fingernails. You should be able to get that one?

<?> Oh this is great.

–   After this selection, 466 texts containing header information on the four selected fields and speaker identification in the dialogues remained. A file with
this information was created, and a part of it is shown in Table 3.3.

–   The headings of the 466 texts were surveyed and four major groups of types of
interactions were identified and the proportion in which they occurred in the
corpus was calculated:

1.   Texts containing exclusively casual conversation[2] (e.g., friends talking at
home): (53%).

2.   Texts containing a combination of interactions classified as task-related
(e.g., in a pottery class), service encounters (e.g., interaction between a
server and customers in a coffee shop), and casual conversations: (25%).

3.   Texts containing casual conversations and telephone conversations:
(18%).

4.   Texts containing exclusively work-related interactions (e.g., in a business
office): (3%).

Table 3.3 Conversation subcorpus header information

File #	Settings	Types of Interactions	# of Speakers	Ages
158001	Dining room Kitchen	Casual conversation	4	48, 47 ,7, 13
151002	living room, bedroom	Casual / phone conversation	2	37, 32
156102	Law firm; copy room	Casual conversation / task-related	9	20, 41, 21, 17, ?, 27, ?, 30, 21
160201	Hotel room, car, restaurant	Casual conversation / service encounter	4	51, 50, 46, 45
125303	Business office	Various work-related	3	55,45, 19

---

2.   The headers of the American conversation corpus identify these casual conversations as
face-to-face conversations. I prefer to call them *casual conversations* because, essentially, except
for telephone talks, all of the other speech types (e.g., work-related, service encounters) are
technically face-to-face, but perhaps not as casual.

Table 3.4 Composition of the American English conversation subcorpus

Types of Interactions	# of texts	# of words	Average # of words per text
Casual conversation	38	312,807	8,232
Task-related / service en-counters /casual	19	152,819	8,043
Phone / casual conversa-tions	16	108,347	6,771
Work-related only	2	15,749	7,874
Complete subcorpus	**75**	**589,722**	7,863

There were no texts that contained task-related, service encounters, or telephone conversations exclusively. The final selection of texts was made according to this proportion. Table 3.4 shows the final composition of the American English conversation subcorpus. In addition to the number of texts that make up each of the speech type groups, Table 3.4 shows the total number of words per group of types of interactions and the average number of words for each text in each of the four categories. These 75 texts containing a total of 589,722 words were utilized for analysis and are from now on referred to as the *conversation corpus*.

3.2.5 The Conversation corpus: Settings and interactions

The overall analysis of settings and interactions within the four interaction types in the conversation corpus was based on the information contained in the headers and qualitative analysis of several segments of dialogues. In the following sections, each of these interaction types is described and exemplified. A summary of the settings where these interactions take place is also provided.

3.2.5.1 *Casual conversations*

The American English conversation portion of the *Longman Grammar Corpus* contains a group of texts identified as face-to-face conversation (to which I refer to as *casual conversation*, see footnote 2). These interactions are exchanges between family members and close friends. Unlike the interactional characteristics of *Friends*, casual conversations take place in several different settings and present a wide range of types of interactions and/or conversation topics. The summary in Table 3.5 shows over ten different settings (e.g., bedroom, café, small restaurant, in the car) and several types of interactions (e.g., visiting with aunt, babysitting, playing games).

Table 3.5 Summary of settings/types of interactions in casual conversations

Settings	Types of interactions
Home/bedroom	Chit-chat/gossip
Kitchen	Visiting with aunt; sitting in kitchen after dinner
Apartment/bedroom	Coming over to spend the night; watching TV before speakers go to bed
Café, parking lot	Women meeting at Starbuck's for coffee
Condo/kitchen	Eating dinner and talking afterward
Living/dining room	Babysitting
Family room/dining room/kitchen	Feeding baby, fixing breakfast
Small restaurant	4 women meeting for dinner
At home	Packing; playing games
In the car	Chatting; talking about cultural issues

In addition to this automatic identification of settings and interactions, several dialogues[3] were analyzed and three major interactional patterns relating to purpose and topic were found: discourse immediacy, narrative focus, and extended topics.

Discourse immediacy

Speakers communicate with different interlocutors for different purposes. Interlocutors, purpose, and topic have a direct impact on interactional patterns. Several sections of the dialogues consistently contained interactions in which the participants just refer to what they are doing at the moment. Chafe (1994) calls this interactional pattern "immediate mode."[4] This immediacy refers to occasions in which "people verbalize experiences that are directly related to their immediate environments" (ibid., p. 196). According to Chafe, when speakers interact in the immediate mode, they "[are] focused on events which they perceiv[e], ac[t] upon, and evaluat[e] at the time and place of the conversation itself" (ibid., p. 197). In the following excerpt, the participants are at home packing. Extracts like this are extremely context-dependent. There are no comments about other events and no stories are told.

> *Setting*: At home (file # 130602)
> A: Did you wash these?
> B: I just did honey.

---

3.   To make this task manageable, every fifth text was selected and several different segments of conversations were analyzed.

4.   See Chafe (1994), Chapter 15, for a discussion of what Chafe calls "The Immediate and Displaced Modes in Conversational Language".

A: You didn't take the stickers off? Oh, no.
B: Is this the blue one you are talking about?
C: No. My blue sweats.
B: Do you want to bring this?
C: No.
A: What's that? Is that a short sweatshirt?
B: Yeah. <nv_laugh>
C: No, it's a hooded, like a shirt.
A: <nv_clears throat>
B: This might, this is small to pack.
C: No, I don't want to bring these.
A: Did you guys go shopping?
C: Oh, no. I did.
B: Is this the one you are looking for?
C: No. Sweats. Pants.

Narrative focus

Some sections of the dialogues were characterized by a predominance of narrative discourse. This pattern seems to be linked to the amount of time people spend together. After some time – perhaps after the primary communicative purpose of the encounter was accomplished – the participants of casual conversations seem to naturally shift to 'story-telling mode.' The topics of these narratives may be directly related to the previous exchanges or just triggered by something said earlier that reminded one of the speakers of a completely unrelated event. An interesting feature of this type of interaction is the presence of extended turns produced by one of the speakers and non-minimal responses (McCarthy, 2002) (e.g., *Sure*) or instances of backchannel (e.g., *Uh huh*) by the other(s).[5] Notice how, unlike what happens with immediate discourse, the structure of turns is uneven, with one of the speakers offering a much longer contribution to the interaction.

In the excerpt below, one of the speakers starts talking about Disneyland, how clean it is, and how they take care of children there. This reminds her of a partially related event and she starts to describe it. This part of the dialogue has several instances of linguistic features typically associated with narrative discourse (Biber, 1988; Biber, Conrad, & Reppen, 1998): past tense (bold), past perfect aspect (bold and italics), and third-person pronouns (or third person reference) (in italics).

---

5.   These features are defined and discussed later in the book in the chapters in which they are addressed.

Setting: At a café (file # 119201)

C: and, uh, and I, we **passed** *her* and you know how like you register later?

A: <u>Uh huh</u>

C: So we **passed** *her* and then I **said** <unclear> you know, I bet *she's* lost and we **turned** around and just at that time *another woman* somewhat younger than ourselves but not much <unclear> and I could see *she* **was** trying to <unclear> oh, I **heard** *her* say and just then *a woman* comes out <unclear> <mimicking>Oh what are you doing and where **did** you **get** those shoes?</mimicking> <unclear>...*she* probably, *the mom* and *the child* **were** in the shoes store and *the little girl* **was** like picking up boxes, you know how *they* do and stuff and then **realized** *she* **didn't** see *her mother* anymore and **came**, *her mom* **had** probably **moved** on thinking *she* **was** right behind *her*

A: <u>Uh huh, yeah</u>

B: Oh I know how that happens

C: but it **was** so funny, *the little girl* **was** torn, *she* **was** thrilled to death to see *her mother* and scared to death because *she* <laughing>**had** shoes... oh</laughing>

A: <u>Wow</u>

C: *They*'re very beautiful

Extended topics

These are parts of dialogues in which speakers spend a considerable amount of time talking about a single topic. The excerpt below shows a part of a discussion revolving around a computer processor, which accounts for almost 20% of the total length of the text (5,310 words). Interactions such as this never occur in *Friends*.

Setting: At home (file # 122201) (Square brackets [ ] indicate overlap)

B: Three eighty-six is a thirty-two bit.

A: I know, so that's not what we're talking about... most of these, the three eighty-six and the four eighty-six are just <unclear> bits... and it's not the register, it's not the data process it's something else

B: <unclear>

A: I'm sure of it

B: You're sure there are eight bits? Atari is eight bits... Atari <unclear> nineteen eighty... those are eight bits.

A: It might be sixteen, but I don't think so... I know they're not thirty-two... I mean this is just something that's

B: <unclear> thirty-two what? You want [thirty-two bits <unclear>]

A: [I don't know, I don't know] what... I don't know <shouting>what</shouting> but look in the, look in the ads and it'll say how many bits.

A: Where... where? It doesn't say bits anywhere... nobody knows what a bit is.

C: Six hundred bits <unclear>

A: <nv_laugh>

B: Sound card... sound card... that's just purely for the sound... sixteen, sixteen bit <unclear> for the sound card.

A: Alright I'm sorry, David, I don't know what it is I, I'm referring to but I know...

B: Your processor

A: [<unclear>]

B: [the four eighty six processor] has a thirty-two bit data buss.

A: I'm not arguing that.

B: Thirty-two bit registers.

A: I'm not arguing that... I'm arguing that there's another criterion and that the other criteria is only eight bit your [processor]

B: [Eighty]

A: processor

B: There's an eight bit processor?

A: Yes.

B: Like <unclear> processor or something?

A: No, main processor.

3.2.5.2 *Task-related, service encounters, and casual conversations*

A group of texts in the conversation corpus contained three interaction types. Examples of task-related interactions include those taking place in a school in which the instructor guides students in a pottery class (i.e., gives instructions) and those taking place at home in which the participants engage in a conversation focused on making Christmas cookies; examples of service encounters include interactions at the registrar's office (where students registering for classes interact with an attendant) and those in a restaurant as speakers interact with servers. Table 3.6 shows a summary of these types of interactions. Casual conversations were discussed above and are not included here.

Table 3.6 Summary of settings/types of interactions in texts containing task-related and service encounters

Settings	Types of interactions
University building / board room	Requesting money from Program Board for their events
Study room	Students studying, checking out books
Faculty office	Discussion of collaborative article
Office	Two people discussing potential grant project with the supervisor
Small office space	Interacting with co-workers and supervisors
Community college / pottery room	In a pottery class
Columbia Basin College	Registration
Dining room	Making Christmas cookies
Academic building	Several people are being trained as "party associates"

Compared to texts classified as casual conversations, these interactions present a different group of settings, ranging from a faculty's office in a university to a study room to the pottery room at a community college. In the excerpt below, students are talking about a school-related subject in a rather informal way.

> *Setting*: Study room (file # 119001)
> B: Right... yeah, I know, I know that much... but I was just trying to find who some of these gods are... I mean like, because I can't remember a lot of them, like Pan... I'm like uh
> A: Pan was the little, he's like a half-goat dude... walks around with little panpipes in the forest
> B: Yeah... I know... I just found that out <unclear>
> A: <nv_laugh> I remember him from cartoons... they have him in cartoons all the time... or just some little wood nymph creature... he's like little dungeons and dragons <unclear>... don't ask me, a random thought.
> B: Me? I'm just so, I'm just like staring at things and my eyes are just blurry... maybe its 'cos I need new contacts... oh my God, this story goes on forever.
> A: Which one?
> B: The one about Echo.

In the next excerpt, students are signing up for class. As part of the interaction, the attendant is asked for information and gives instructions. The exchange is typically transactional, being limited to requests and exchange of information. Overall the interactions in task-related conversations and service encounters tend to have an informational focus. Sometimes, the exchange of information takes place while a task is being performed, as in file # 119001, above; at other times, requests are made and instructions are given, as in the service encounter in file # 144701, below.

Setting: At Columbia Basin College, registrar's office (file # 144701)

A: Okay.

B: Okay, I make sure of the class I am in and where it's at.

A: Okay, what does it say on your slip?

B: Uh, well, it's said W one thirteen but now it says R one O three on here. And that is the original paperwork.

A: Yeah, it is.

B: So how do I check on that?

A: I don't know you can talk to that lady right behind you. She is the one that handles the schedules. I don't know why it got changed but she can help you.

B: Thank you.

A: Uh huh. <nv_sigh>

B: Right there ma'am. The lady on the phone.

A: Can I get my schedule changed?

A: Yeah you sure can.

B: How long do they take to get.

A: About two minutes.

B: Oh all right. <nv_laugh> I thought I would have to pick it up the next day or something.

A: No we're fast. Okay, I do not know who filled this out. It looks like you wrote this like you wrote this. See this line number right here?

B: Uh huh.

3.2.5.3 *Texts with phone conversations and casual conversations*

This set of texts is characterized by casual conversations (with the same characteristics described in Section 3.2.5.1) interrupted by occasional phone conversations. Table 3.7 displays a summary of the settings and types of interactions (similar to those related to texts with exclusively casual conversations) in this group of texts.

Table 3.7 Summary of settings/types of interactions in texts with phone and casual conversations

Settings	Types of interactions
Living room	Relaxing in the living room; chatting over the phone
Restaurant / home	Having lunch with father; at home with mother and on the phone
Kitchen / living room	Preparing dinner, eating, talking on phone
Alterations shop	Conversation / phone call while workers are sewing
Private home	Family chit-chat; phone conversation

Most telephone conversations show only one side of the dialogue (just a few are on the speaker phone). These 'monologues' tend to be long and so context-dependent that their topics can be hard to understand. These phone exchanges, when long and not intended to just elicit or provide some specific information, share one of the interactional patterns typical of casual conversations (narrative focus) in that they are also interspersed with narrative accounts. The extract below takes place at home. Several instances of past tense (in bold) are found in this narrative part of the interaction.

> *Setting*: At home (file # 149901)[6]
> <tel> Yes it's my fault...(6) Mhm... Michael and I **spent** the day at <unclear> and we **drove** home in fog at night and it **took** us like, it **took** me an hour and a half to get home... Yeah...(3) Uh huh... And not only that, like by the time I **started** to get places, like there **was** a power line down Wisconsin Ave, so they wouldn't let anyone drive down Wisconsin Ave and I'm like, it **was** a nightmare, so I'm <unclear> **got** home by <unclear> nine thirty <unclear> I **was** supposed to meet Beth out and it **was** like, forget it. <nv_laugh> <nv_sniff> So...(4) Uh huh...(3) You're kidding... Oh...(8) Mhm...(5) **Was** it? <nv_sigh> Yeah, the snow...(5) Mhm...(7) Mhm...(5) It **was**, yeah, it **was** a bad night... **Did** you **lose** power?... Oh, that's good... Yeah... We **lost** power. I **thought** we **were** going to freeze.

3.2.5.4 *Texts with work-related conversations*

Exclusively work-related interactions are rare in the *Longman Grammar Conversation Corpus*. Most of these interactions occur in a business office. The participants exchange information and comment on events relating to what they are doing at the moment or past events directly associated with the task they are performing or discussing. This type of interaction is illustrated in the extract below.

---

6.   The numbers in parentheses indicate the time elapsed (in seconds) between turns.

Setting: In a business office (file #125101)

A: How much has <unclear> given up to this point?

B: Uh eighteen I think.

A: What do the invitations look like?

B: They're right there as you walk in uh uh they're fine I think. Still wasn't quite clear to me who uh who made the error you know the as she said they're uh

A: That's yeah that's not the blue I picked

B: Blue?

A: This [is]

B: [nothing blue about it]

A: Yeah. I don't know if this is this doesn't look as bad as the baby poop color that they had picked out

B: No

A: It may be though the same one that he wanted and I picked out the blue

B: [That is not blue]

A: [and he just wanted the one he wanted]

B: [that's just yeah]

A: [he just didn't want blue I don't think I guess]. When I went over there to pick out this color and

A: Did you tell <unclear>

B: Uh huh

Similar to task-related interactions, work-related interactions also involve exchanges of information, requests, and instructions. These interactions, overall, are focused on the task at hand and tend to give little room for personal accounts.

3.3 Settings and interactions: *Friends* versus conversation

This brief analysis of the overall characteristics of the types of settings and interactions in the two corpora reveals that *Friends* presents a much more limited number of settings and a much narrower range of types of interactions/topics. The most frequent settings in *Friends* are *Central Perk*, a coffee house where the characters meet on a regular basis (and where several episodes begin and end) and the places where they live (especially Monica and Rachel's apartment). Most of the conversations revolve around the themes of friendship, dating, and sex. In addition to this restricted number of settings and topics, most dialogues in *Friends* tend to refer to immediate problems or events. In the television show, the scenes change constantly, and the characters frequently arrive in places (especially at the beginning of scenes). This situational circumstance results in several exchanges where the characters meet, producing a large number of greetings.

In contrast, the conversation corpus features a much wider range of settings and interactions/topics. In addition to casual interactions, the conversation corpus has task- and work-related exchanges, interactions in service encounters, and telephone conversations. Casual conversations, which account for most of the interactions in the conversation corpus, show a combination of different characteristics related to purpose and topic, which I classified as: discourse immediacy, narrative focus, and extended topics. The exchanges containing narrative segments often co-occur with extended turns and non-minimal responses or instances of backchannel, making these turns unequally distributed. The dialogues in *Friends*, on the other hand, tend to focus on immediate discourse with rare instances of lopsided turns.

3.4 Data coding and concordancing

Both corpora were annotated for parts of speech and grammatical features using an automatic grammatical tagger developed by Douglas Biber at Northern Arizona University[7]. Perfected over a period of 10 years, the *Biber Tagger* is a software program that 'tags' texts for over 100 linguistic features. This grammatical annotation makes it possible to search for grammatical features (e.g., instances of first-person pronouns, nouns, present tense verbs) or a combination of lexical items and grammatical features in a corpus. For example, to search for instances of the noun *date* (as in *I have a date tonight.*), the tag for *nouns* is added (i.e., date ^nn+++). By the same token, to search for the verb *date*, the search is done for *date* followed by the tag for verbs (i.e., date ^vb+++). Below is an excerpt of a tagged text; each tag is followed by its description.

I	^pp1a+pp1+++	[1st person personal pronoun]
have	^vb+hv+vrb++	[Have as main verb]
a	^at++++	[Indefinite article]

---

7. The American English conversation corpus was tagged to facilitate the search for and comparison of individual features, most of which presented in the subsequent chapters. The comparison of the multidimensional analysis of *Friends* (see Chapter 4) is made relative to the results of Biber's (1988) study, which is typically done in several other multidimensional studies (see especially Conrad & Biber, 2001). For the sake of curiosity, though, I ran the American English conversation subcorpus through Biber's *Tag Count*. The score obtained by the American conversation corpus on dimension 1 (involved vs. informational production) was very similar to the results of Biber's (1988) study, confirming the findings in Helt (2001) according to which face-to-face British and American English conversation do not present salient differences along Biber's dimension 1.

date   ^nn++++   [Singular noun]

tonight ^nr+tm+++   [Time adverbial noun]

All of the searches for linguistic features (see Appendix for a complete list) were done automatically using a concordance software program, MonoConc Pro 2.2 (Barlow, 2002) and were manually checked for accuracy and disambiguation purposes when necessary. Concordance programs display the occurrences of a particular word, linguistic feature, or a combination of both with their surrounding context. Each of these occurrences is called a KWIC, *Key Word In Context*. Typically, each occurrence of a particular item (e.g., a word) is displayed in a single line with the searched feature in the middle and context on both sides. Figure 3.1 shows the result for the search for '*kind of.*'

This particular concordancer displays the KWICs in the larger window. Clicking on a particular occurrence of the searched term (the third line in this example) will prompt the smaller upper window to show more context. This way, different meanings (or word classes) can be identified. In this example, I was searching for instances of the hedge *kind of*, as in the first line (i.e., *kind of nebulous*). However, the search produced instances of the noun *kind* with the meaning of *type*, as in the

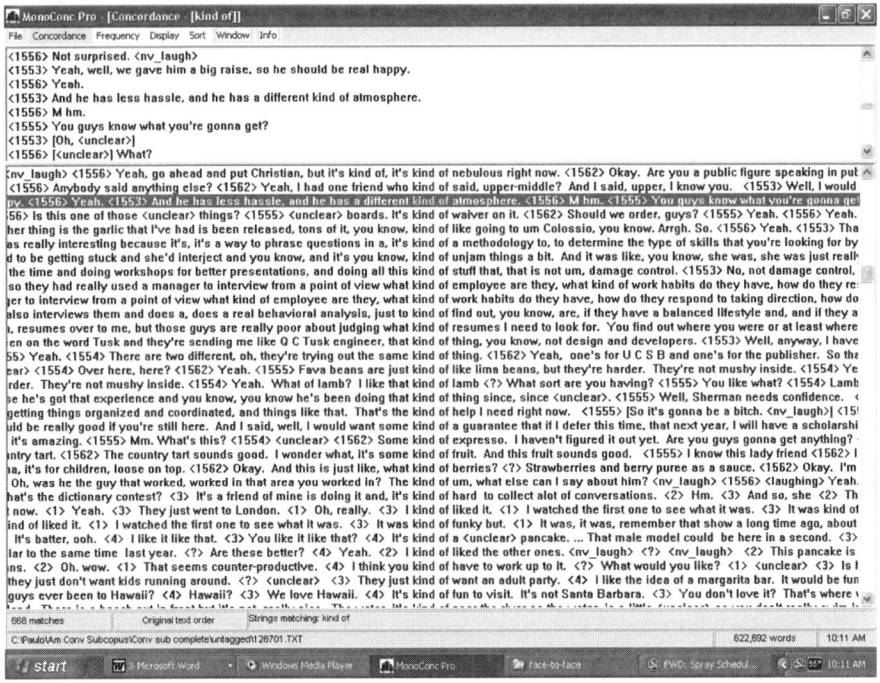

Figure 3.1 Sample Key Word in Context (KWIC) concordance lines for kind of.

ninth line (i.e., *what kind of employee are they*). Therefore, after the initial automatic search, all the concordance lines were read and only the instances of hedges were kept for analysis.

Concordancers also allow searches for grammatical features using tagged texts. For example, the search for past tense occurrences was done by entering the tag for past tense (i.e., vbd+++xvbn+ in the *Biber Tagger*). Even though the *Biber Tagger* has a very high accuracy rate (up to 97% depending on the register), there were cases in which the data had to be manually checked for accuracy. This was done several times when the searched items were potentially ambiguous. For example, the adjective *cool* was tagged correctly in 100% of the instances but had to be checked manually for disambiguation, as only its slangy meaning (e.g., great, fashionable – as in *What a cool job!)* was included in the analysis.

Another example of the need for manual disambiguation involving the tagged versions of the corpora was the case of the lexical and copular *get*, as in examples (1) and (2) respectively.

(1)   She was kinda saying, maybe I should <u>get</u> a job 'cause she was feeling like out of touch. (Conversation)

(2)   Rachel: Oh God, I just <u>got</u> so nervous that he would say no. (*Friends*)

The frequency of copular *get* was initially based on the instances of *get*[8] followed by an adjective, as reported in LGSWE (p. 438). Using the concordancer, this search was done by entering the different forms of *get* plus the verb tag followed by any word (indicated by the wild card '*') that had been tagged as an adjective: get ^vb++++ * ^jj++++. As example (2) above shows, instances of copular *get* in which the verb was separated by one or two words (usually hedges or adverbial intensifiers) were being missed. For accuracy purposes, the searches for copular *get* were done in three complementary steps: *get* followed by zero, one, and two words before the adjective. Obviously, all of these occurrences had to be checked individually, so that instances such as (3) were correctly classified and included in the analysis, and instances such as (4) were excluded.

(3)   …And it <u>got</u> so very <u>difficult</u> for me, and then I realized that I was not well. (Conversation)

(4)   Chandler: … I <u>got</u> a <u>big</u> dinosaur bone to inspect. (*Friends*)

---

8.   It should be noted that by saying instances of *get*, I mean *get, gets, getting* (*gettin'*), *got*, and *gotten*.

3.5 Norming

When comparing corpora of different sizes, the raw frequency of linguistic features must be normed (or normalized) to a common base to allow for accurate comparisons. For example, the complete American English conversation corpus yielded 4169 occurrences of the adverbial *actually*; in *Friends*, only 632 instances of this adverbial were found. The complete conversation corpus, however, has approximately 4,000,000 words, and *Friends* has about 600,000 words. To norm these counts to a rate of occurrences (e.g., frequency per 1,000,000 words), the raw frequency of the feature is divided by the total number of words in the corpus and then multiplied by 1,000,000:

(Raw frequency / total number of words in the corpus) X base

Therefore, for the conversation corpus:

(4169 / 4,000,000) X 1,000,000 = **1042.2** occurrences per million words

For the *Friends* corpus:

(632 / 600,000) X 1,000,000 = **1053.3** occurrences per million words

After the raw counts are normalized, therefore, we see that the conversation corpus produced 1042.2 occurrences of *actually* per million words; *Friends* yielded 1053.3 instances of *actually*. This shows that the initial impression (that *actually* is much more frequent in conversation than in *Friends*) did not prove to be true: the use of *actually* in conversation and *Friends* is, actually, almost identical, with *Friends* presenting a slightly higher frequency of this feature.

As I mentioned earlier, norming is required for comparisons of corpora of different sizes. For the present study, however, both corpora (the *Friends* corpus and the conversation subcorpus) are almost identical in size, which makes norming unnecessary. I decided, nonetheless, to norm all frequencies to a base of 1,000,000 words so as to facilitate comparisons with other studies, which typically report results in tokens per million words.

3.6 Statistical significance

Several statistical significance tests are used in corpus-based studies depending on the nature of the analysis. For the co-occurrence of specific lexical words (i.e., collocations) or lexical words and grammatical structures (i.e., colligations), the mutual information, t, and z tests are commonly used. For the comparison of raw frequencies of features in a corpus or in different corpora, the chi-square or log-likelihood scores are often used (see McEnery, Xiao, & Tono (2006), pp. 52–58 for a discussion of statistical significance in corpus linguistics; see also Oakes (1998) for an excellent book-length description of statistics in corpus linguistics).

These tests assist researchers with the interpretation of the relative importance of frequency differences, which may suggest, for example, salient functional differences between two registers or point to phenomena of language change in progress in diachronic analyses. For example, McEnery and Xiao (2005b) examined the use of the verb *help* followed by a bare infinitive (as in *She helped me do it* -- as opposed to *She helped me to do it*) in written British English over a period of three decades (1961–1991). In this case study based on the Lancaster-Oslo-Bergen corpus of British English (LOB corpus) and the Freiburg-LOB corpus of British English (FLOB corpus), the researchers used the log-likelihood technique to test for significance and reported (among other findings) that the use of *help* followed by a bare infinitive has significantly increased over time in British English.

The comparison of a single linguistic feature across corpora is much more straightforward than the comparison of groups of features. Also using the log-likelihood test, I report the significance of individual features (e.g., use of hedges in *Friends* and in conversation) in the Appendix. Even though I report the results of the comparison of features in frequency per million words throughout the book, I used raw frequencies to test for significance because, as noted by McEnery, Xiao, and Tono (2006), proportional data (such as normed counts) should not be used in either chi-square or log-likelihood tests[9]. However, I do not rely on the significance tests in the interpretation of the results because I consider the statistical significance of individual features secondary to the overall *tendency* suggested by the groups of linguistic features sharing the same or similar discourse functions.

For example, the analysis of emotional language (Chapter 6) includes several linguistic features associated with emotional content. *All* followed by an adjective (as in *She was all happy* and *She was all crying*) was one of these features. Even though the comparison between *Friends* and conversation did not show a statistically significant difference in the use of this feature, it was nonetheless included in the analysis as a *contributing* feature defining an overall tendency toward this function (emotional language) in *Friends*. I therefore interpret the results from a broader perspective in which the whole (the big picture) is greater than the individual sum of its parts.

---

9.   I used the log-likelihood test instead of chi-square for two reasons: several comparisons involved very high frequencies and, as Oakes (1998) points out, the higher the frequency counts, the more likely it is that the chi-square test will show significance; the second reason is that the log-likelihood does not assume a normal distribution (Dunning, 1993; McEnery, Xiao, & Tono, 2006; Oates, 1998). For more information on the use of the chi-square and log-likelihood statistics in corpus linguistics, see Rayson, Berridge, and Francis (2004) and Rayson and Garside (2000).

3.7 Functional differences

Chapter 4 focuses on multidimensional analysis (Biber, 1988), comparing *Friends* to conversation on Biber's Dimension 1 (*involved vs. informational production*). In a nutshell, Chapter 4 is about the linguistic similarities between the two corpora.

A closer look at the frequency counts, however, indicated that, despite the overall high frequency of conversational features, some of them tended to be consistently more frequent in one of the two corpora. The linguistic features showing important differences in frequency counts were grouped functionally according to the discourse patterns that emerged from the analysis. For example, linguistic features associated with vague language such as hedges (e.g., *sort of*) and nouns of vague reference (e.g., *stuff*) were consistently higher in conversation. These features are then the object of analysis of Chapter 5 on *vague language*; features reflecting emotional language/emphatic content, such as adverbial intensifiers (e.g., *so*), emphatic *do* (as in *I do love you*), and certain expletives (e.g., *damn*) were consistently higher in *Friends*. Chapter 6, on *emotional language*, focuses on the analysis of these features.

These groupings of linguistic features are the basis for the analyses presented in Chapters 5 through 8. It should be noted, however, that particular linguistic features may be associated with different discourse functions. For example, the adverbial intensifier *so* is associated with emotional language and is primarily analyzed as an adjective modifier (e.g., *so* beautiful) in Chapter 6; in addition to this emphatic function, *so* is described as one of the innovative linguistic features of American English conversation associated with informality (e.g., an adverbial intensifier modifying a noun, as in *This is <u>so</u> your fault*), and is analyzed as such in Chapter 7.

The inclusion of the same feature as representative of different functions may at times be somewhat confusing. As I indicated in Chapter 1 in the description of the 'discourse circumstances of conversation' (fully discussed in LGSWE, Chapter 14), these circumstances (shared context, avoidance of elaboration of meaning, interactiveness, real-time production, expression of stance) are inherently interconnected and interdependent. For example, because speakers rely on shared context and sometimes due to the pressures of real-time production, they avoid elaboration of meaning which, in turn, contributes to and reflects the interactive nature of conversation. As a result, linguistic features such as hedges (e.g., *kind of, sort of*), *primarily* associated with vague language, also make an important contribution to the interactiveness of conversational exchanges. The apparent imprecision that these hedges suggest functions as an invitation for the interlocutor to contribute to the communicative event – either by asking for clarification or participating in the co-construction of meaning initiated by the other speaker. For this reason, I believe it is important to resort to this 'double dipping,' which ultimately is a reflection of the integrative nature of language in general and of conversation in particular.

3.8 The choice of linguistic features

The Appendix lists all of the linguistic features involved in the present study. Overall, this selection was based on a survey of LGSWE, especially Chapter 14, *The Grammar of Conversation*. As Rühlemann (2007) acknowledges, this chapter "provides an account of the workings of spoken grammar that is as yet unparalleled in its breadth and depth" (p. 11). Other features were included based on frequency or my personal research interest. The inclusion of the noncanonical use of the adverbial intensifier *so* modifying a verb, as in *We're so gonna party* (*Friends*) (although relatively infrequent when compared to its canonical use, so + adjective), and the innovative use of *totally* as an expression of emphatic agreement, as in *Phoebe: He's holding us back. Ross: Totally!* (*Friends*) are two such examples.

Once the overall functional differences were identified, practical decisions had to be made in the selection process. Keeping in mind that the primary purpose of the present study is to compare the language of *Friends* to natural conversation (not to provide a comprehensive account of conversation), some potentially interesting features had to be discarded because of the difficulty of automatically identifying them and providing accurate frequency counts. A case in point is the use of *like* as a hedge, as in *normally it doesn't make you feel full though 'cause it's so like filling* (Conversation). Because *like* can have several different grammatical functions, automatic tagging is not as accurate as with other linguistic features. This means that the 6300 instances of *like* found in the conversation subcorpus would have to be checked manually, which would be impractical. In addition, other features sharing the same or similar discourse functions, such as *kind of like*, were more easily identifiable.

Finally, the analysis of similarities and differences between the two corpora was based on overall frequency counts. A decision relative to breadth and depth of analysis also had to be made. Instead of engaging in elaborate discussions of a few linguistic features, I, in large part, provide a descriptive account of a large number of features (close to 100) with numerous examples and direct the reader to other in-depth studies of particular features when pertinent.

3.9 Summary

In this chapter, the methodology used in the present study was presented and topics such as concordancing, automatic grammatical annotation, norming, and statistical significance were addressed. The two corpora were thoroughly described, including a brief analysis of the most common settings and types of interactions/topics in each corpus. This description revealed that *Friends* presents a very limited number of settings (as compared to conversation) and a much narrower set of interaction types and topics, which are usually restricted to friendship, romantic relationships, dating, and sex.

The concept of functional differences was also introduced. Despite the high frequency of conversational features that pervade both corpora (see Chapter 4), a closer frequency-based analysis of these features indicated that those sharing particular discourse functions (e.g., vague language) tended to be consistently more frequent in one of the corpora, thus functionally characterizing each corpus. These groupings of features provide the framework for comparisons and are presented in Chapters 5 through 8. Finally, the rationale for the choice of linguistic features included in the study and the reason for the 'double dipping' of certain features were explained.

In the next chapter, I describe multidimensional analysis (Biber, 1988), which is an integral part of the methodology utilized in the present study. For ease of reference, the methodology and the results of the multidimensional analysis of *Friends* are presented together in Chapter 4.

Take 1

Dimensions and similarities

Rachel: Hey... Hi <u>you</u> guys! Listen, <u>you</u> know what? <u>I</u>'<u>m</u> not feeling <u>really</u> well. <u>I</u> <u>think</u> <u>I</u> <u>can</u>'<u>t</u> get out for the play.

Ross: Really? Wh-what'<u>s</u> wrong?

Rachel: <u>I</u> <u>don</u>'<u>t</u> know! <u>I</u> <u>think</u> <u>it</u>'<u>s</u> <u>kind of</u> serious! <u>Oh</u>, <u>you</u> know... <u>I</u> was watching this thing on TV this morning about... Newcastle disease... and <u>I</u> <u>think</u> <u>I</u> might have it!!

Charlie: <u>Oh</u>, Newcastle disease <u>is</u> a secretion borne virus that only affe<u>cts</u> chickens and... other poultry.

Rachel: ...<u>Ok</u>, who <u>is</u> <u>this</u>?

Ross: <u>I</u>'<u>m</u> sorry, Rachel, <u>this</u> <u>is</u> Charlie Wealer, she'<u>s</u> a colleague.

Rachel: <u>Oh</u>, hi! <u>I</u> would shake <u>your</u> hand but... <u>I</u>'<u>m</u> sure <u>you</u> <u>don</u>'<u>t</u> <u>want</u> to get <u>my</u> chicken disease!

(*Friends: Season 9, episode 20: The One with the Soap Opera Party*)

A: What? What <u>are</u> <u>you</u> talking <u>about</u>?

B: <u>You</u> <u>can</u>'<u>t</u> do what?

A: Baby-sit

B: Then <u>I</u> <u>can</u>'<u>t</u> either. If <u>you</u> <u>can</u>'<u>t</u> go she wanted me

A: <u>I</u> <u>don</u>'<u>t</u> <u>know</u> <u>I</u>'<u>ll</u> have to figure something out.

B: <u>Okay</u> <u>well</u> <u>I</u> <u>think</u> <u>I</u>'<u>m</u> going to go for a walk. <u>I</u> feel <u>so</u> fat, <u>I</u> ate <u>so</u> much at lunch.

A: How many tacos?

B: <u>I</u> <u>just</u> had one but then <u>I</u> had a few chips and then <u>I</u> had ice cream pie, <u>I</u> should<u>n</u>'<u>t</u> have had that ice cream pie…

(*Conversation: Longman Grammar Corpus*)

4.1 Introduction

In this chapter, I provide a brief description of Multidimensional (MD) analysis (Biber, 1988) and present a summary of the results of Biber's study of register variation. Then, applying Biber's MD framework, I compare *Friends* to conversation on Dimension 1, *involved vs. informational production*.[1] I show that *Friends* shares the core linguistic features of conversation. The two excerpts from *Friends* and conversation that open this chapter have several of the linguistic features that characterize involved registers such as face-to-face conversation: among other features, they have several instances of first- and second-person pronouns, private verbs (think), contractions, present tense verbs, and discourse particles (*Oh, Okay*). Features such as these are the object of analysis of this chapter.

4.2 Multidimensional analysis: A brief introduction

Multidimensional (MD) analysis is a quantitative corpus-based technique designed to find and interpret the co-occurrence of certain linguistic features in a corpus. As Biber, Conrad, Reppen, Byrd, and Helt (2002) explain, "on the assumption that co-occurrence reflects shared functions, analysts interpret the co-occurrence patterns to assess the situational, social, and cognitive functions most widely shared by the linguistic features" (p. 14).

Biber (1988) conducted a linguistic study of register variation in English. He hypothesized that different registers (e.g., face-to-face conversation, fiction, academic prose) would reveal different co-occurrence patterns of linguistic features and that these co-occurrence patterns would reflect the major communicative functions of these registers. To accomplish the goal of the study, a series of steps were taken. I outline these steps here in a very simplified manner:

Step 1: Based on previous research, a large number of linguistic features associated with different functions of the language were chosen. For example, first- and second-person pronouns, contractions, and demonstrative pronouns have been associated with interactive discourse (e.g., conversation) and shared context. Passive voice and nominalizations have been associated with more formal registers (e.g., academic prose). Linguistic features such as these were good candidates for the analysis. It should be noted, however, that it was not assumed that these features necessarily reflected the functions attributed to them in previous research. They were just part of a large pool of features to be used in the analysis (see Biber, 1988, pp. 73–75, for a complete list of these features).

Step 2: A large number of texts representing a wide range of functions of English were selected. Biber used two major corpora for the analysis: the Lancaster-

---

1.   Of all the dimensions discussed in Biber (1988), Dimension 1 (involved vs. informational production) is the strongest and most stable. Further, this dimension deals specifically with conversation. For this reason, I focus my analysis on Biber's Dimension 1.

Oslo-Bergen Corpus of British English (LOB corpus) and the London-Lund Corpus of Spoken English (LLC corpus). The first corpus is composed of 500 written texts of about 2,000 words each taken from fifteen genres (e.g., press reportage, editorials, official documents); the second corpus comprises 87 texts of spoken British English containing about 5,000 words each, representing six speech situations (e.g., private conversations, radio broadcasts, prepared speeches).

Step 3: Once the texts were selected, they were automatically annotated for the grammatical features chosen in step 1 (see Chapter 3, Section 3.4 on grammatical annotation).

Step 4: The quantitative analysis of the data was carried with *Factor Analysis*. In corpus linguistics, this statistical procedure uses frequency counts of linguistic features to identify sets of features that co-occur in texts. For example, features such as past tense verbs, third person pronouns, and public verbs (e.g., *say, admit*) were found to co-occur with high frequencies.

Step 5: Finally, Biber identified 5 major dimensions of English[2] through the interpretation of "the communicative functions most widely shared by the set of co-occurring features defining [each] dimension" (Biber, Conrad, & Reppen, 1998, p. 149). Going back to the example I used in step 4, the co-occurrence of past tense verbs, third person pronouns, and public verbs was interpreted as defining a textual *dimension* characterized by narrative discourse.

4.3 Results of Biber's (1988) MD analysis

Table 4.1 shows the summary of the co-occurrence patterns underlying the five major dimensions of variation of English (i.e., involved versus informational production, narrative versus non-narrative discourse, elaborated versus situation-dependent reference, overt expression of argumentation, and impersonal versus non-impersonal style). The numbers following the linguistic features represent their factor loading on the dimension, which varies from 1.0 to –1.0. The features with higher loadings are better representatives of the dimension they define. For example, on Dimension 1 (D1), involved versus informational production, private verbs (e.g., think, believe), *that*-deletion, contractions, present tense verbs, and second-person pronouns (the positive features of the dimension) tend to co-occur with high frequencies and are associated with interactive texts (e.g., face-to-face

---

2.   Biber identified seven dimensions of English variation in his 1988 study. Dimension 6 (*On-line informational elaboration marking stance*) and Dimension 7 (*Academic hedging*) have few linguistic features with important loadings and are thus difficult to interpret. Most studies based on Biber's (1988) study do not include these dimensions.

conversation). On the other hand, the features below the dashed line (e.g., nouns, prepositions, attributive adjectives), called negative features, tend to *not* co-occur with the positive features. The positive and negative features are thus said to be in complementary distribution. In other words, reflecting the functions of the negative features, for example, informational texts (e.g., academic prose) tend to present a higher frequency of nouns, prepositions, and attributive adjectives and a lower frequency of private verbs or contractions. In the example below, *successful, main,* and *high* are attributive adjectives; *contributing* also has an adjectival function and is used attributively; *germination* and *establishment* are examples of nominalizations (i.e., abstract nouns formed from verbs).

It is well recognized that a <u>successful</u> <u>germination</u> and <u>establishment</u> is one of the <u>main contributing</u> factors governing <u>high</u> yields. (Academic prose, *Longman Grammar Corpus*)

As mentioned above, the scores following each grammatical feature in Table 4.1 represent the importance of the feature in defining a particular dimension. Biber computed mean dimension scores for all of the registers included in the study (see Biber, 1988, pp. 93–97, for a detailed explanation of how the scores were computed). These mean dimension scores are "a summation of the frequencies for those features having salient loads on a dimension" (Biber, Conrad, Reppen, Byrd, & Helt, 2002, p. 17).

Figure 4.1 shows the mean scores for nine registers on D1 (*involved versus informational production*). Face-to-face conversation obtained a score of 35 and is one of the most involved (interactive) registers (next to telephone conversations on the top extreme); on the other end, academic prose was ranked as one the most informational registers (close to official documents) with a score of -15.

The high score obtained by face-to-face conversation on D1 indicates that this register is linguistically characterized by a high frequency of the grammatical features with the highest loadings on this dimension, shown in Table 4.1. Face-to-face conversation, therefore, is characterized by the co-occurrence of features such as private verbs, *that*-deletion, contractions, and first- and second- person pronouns, as illustrated by the dialogue excerpt shown at the beginning of this chapter.

Table 4.1 Summary of the co-occurrence patterns underlying the five major dimensions of English (From Biber, 1988)

Dimension 1: "Involved versus informa-		syntactic negation	.40
tional production"		present participial clauses	.39
private verbs	.96	present tense verbs	-.47
that-deletion	.91	attributive adjectives	-.41
contractions	.90		
present tense verbs	.86	*Dimension 3: "Elaborated versus situa-*	
second-person pronouns	.86	*tion-dependent reference"*	
do as pro-verb	.82	wh-relative clauses	
analytic negation	.78	on object positions	.63
demonstrative pronouns	.76	pied-piping constructions	.61
general emphatics	.74	wh-relative clauses	
first-person pronouns	.74	on subject positions	.45
pronoun *it*	.71	phrasal coordination	.36
be as main verb	.71	nominalizations	.36
causative subordination	.66	time adverbials	-.60
discourse particles	.66	place adverbials	-.49
indefinite pronouns	.62	adverbs	-.46
general hedges	.58		
amplifiers	.56	*Dimension 4: "Overt expression of"*	
sentence relatives	.55	*argumentation*	
wh-questions	.52	infinitives	.76
possibility modals	.50	prediction modals	.54
non-phrasal coordination	.48	suasive verbs	.49
wh-clauses	.47	conditional subordination	.47
final prepositions	.43	necessity modals	.46
adverbs	.42	split auxiliaries	.44
nouns	-.80	possibility modals	.37
word length	-.58	[no negative features]	
prepositions	-.54		
type/token ration	-.54	*Dimension 5: "Impersonal versus non-*	
attributive adjectives	-.47	*impersonal style"*	
place adverbials	-.42	conjuncts	.48
agentless passives	-.39	agentless passives	.43
past participial		past participial adverbial clauses	.42
postnominal clauses	-.38		
		by-passives	.41
		past participial	
Dimension 2: "Narrative versus non-nar-		postnominal clauses	.40
rative discourse"		other adverbial subordinators	.39
past tense verbs	.90	[no negative features]	
third-person pronouns	.73		
perfect aspect verbs	.48		
public verbs	.43		

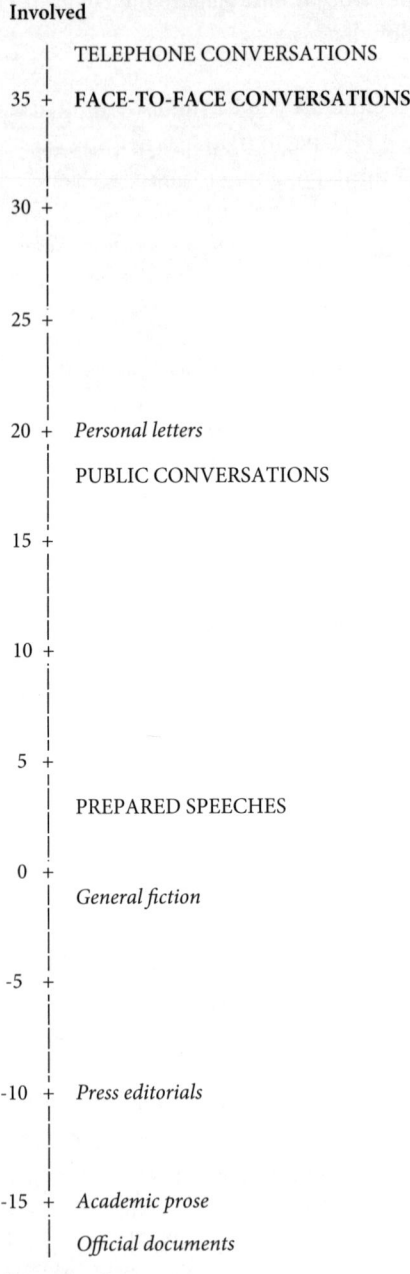

Figure 4.1 Mean scores of English Dimension 1 for nine registers: "Involved versus informational production" (F= 111.9, p <.0001, r^2 = 84.3 percent; spoken registers in small capitals, written registers italicized) (From Biber, Conrad, & Reppen, 1998).

A: What? What are <u>you</u> talking <u>about</u>?

B: <u>You</u> ca<u>n't</u> do what?

A: Baby-sit

B: Then <u>I</u> ca<u>n't</u> either. If <u>you</u> ca<u>n't</u> go she <u>wanted</u> me

A: <u>I</u> do<u>n't</u> <u>know</u> <u>I'll</u> have to figure something out.

B: <u>Okay</u> <u>well</u> <u>I</u> <u>think</u> <u>I'm</u> going to go for a walk. <u>I</u> feel <u>so</u> fat, <u>I</u> ate <u>so</u> much at lunch.

A: How many tacos?

B: <u>I</u> <u>just</u> had one but then <u>I</u> had a few chips and then <u>I</u> had ice cream pie, <u>I</u> should<u>n't</u> have had that ice cream pie…

(*Conversation*: *Longman Grammar Corpus*)

Among other features, this short extract from face-to-face conversation has 11 instances of first- person pronouns (*I*), four private verbs (*want, know, think, feel*), three occurrences of present tense (*don't know, think, feel*), seven contractions (e.g., *can't, don't*), three examples of general emphatics (*just*, two instances of *so*), two discourse particles (*okay, well*), and a stranded preposition (*about*). The co-occurrence of these features indicates that they share similar communicative functions and reflect involvement. In other words, involvement is linguistically realized by high frequencies of these co-occurring features.

As I mentioned earlier, the positive and negative features of D1 are in complementary distribution. Figure 4.1 above shows a *continuum* of registers ranging from highly involved to highly informational. Figure 4.2 provides a graphic representation of the 'movement' of linguistic features along the involved-informational continuum across registers. Each box represents the frequency of the pool of linguistic features typifying the dimension. The gradual movement from casual conversation to official documents is accompanied by the gradual increase and decrease of the frequency of these features.

I used Biber's D1 to illustrate what the dimension scores correspond to linguistically. The same occurs with the other four dimensions: the linguistic features with higher loadings on each dimension are better representatives of the dimension they define. For example, the co-occurrence of past tense verbs, third person pronouns, and perfect aspect verbs (positive features of D2) are typical of narrative discourse. Biber calculated mean dimension scores for each of the registers in his 1988 study on each of the five dimensions. As such, conversation, for example, has a score on D1, another score on D2, and so forth (see Biber, 1988, Chapter 7).

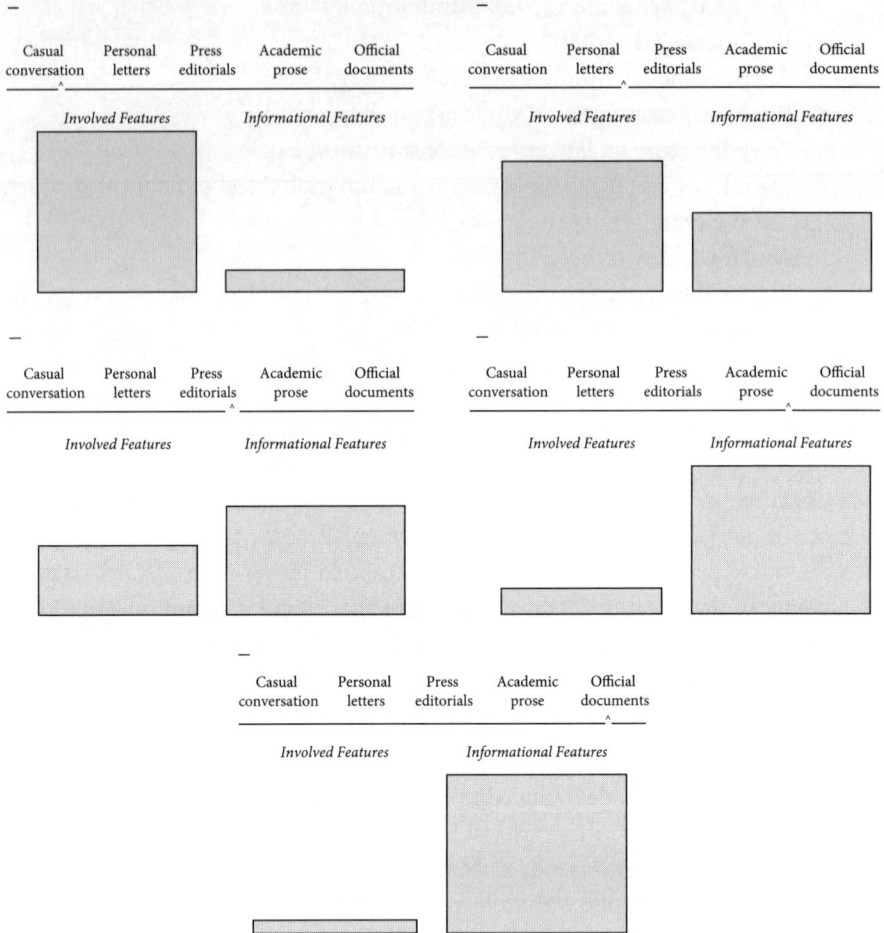

Figure 4.2 Graphic representation of the complementary distribution of linguistic features across registers on dimension 1

The steps outlined in Section 4.2 are followed by researchers intending to carry out a *complete* multidimensional analysis. These researchers choose linguistic features, select and collect texts, annotate them for grammatical features, conduct factor analysis, and then functionally interpret the co-occurrence patterns revealed by the factor analysis. For example, complete MD studies were conducted by Connor-Linton (1989) on crosstalk, White (1994) on the language of job interviews, and Reppen (1994) on elementary school spoken and written registers.

Other studies apply Biber's model of register variation; instead of conducting a *complete* MD, these studies use the dimensions identified in Biber (1988) as the basis for comparisons and descriptions of other registers. For example, Biber's MD model was applied by Conrad (2001) comparing textbooks and journal articles in biology and history, Helt (2001) comparing British and American spoken English, and Rey (2001) in a diachronic investigation of male and female language in the American television series *Star Trek*.

Biber's study is the most comprehensive study of English register variation to date. The results of the analysis provide a benchmark for comparisons with other registers. In the first part of the present study, I use Biber's findings relative to D1 to compare *Friends* to natural conversation.

4.4 The MD analysis of *Friends*

As in the second group of studies mentioned in the previous section, I used Biber's MD model to compare the language of *Friends* to natural conversation. The first step of the study was to collect the *Friends* corpus. The *Friends* corpus comprises transcripts of nine seasons of the show and has approximately 590,000 words (see Chapter 3, Sections 3.2.1–2 for a complete description of the corpus). Once the corpus was collected and saved electronically, it was annotated for grammatical features with the *Biber Tagger*, described in Chapter 3, Section 3.4. After the *Friends* corpus was 'tagged,' it was run through another software program also developed by Douglas Biber (*Tag Count*). This program calculates the frequencies of the linguistic features and computes scores on the five dimensions for each of the texts (i.e., show episodes) that compose the corpus. Finally, the mean score on the five dimensions for the corpus as a whole is calculated.

Table 4.2 shows the descriptive statistics for *Friends* and face-to-face conversation on D1 (*involved versus informational production*). The mean score obtained by *Friends* (34.4) was almost identical to that obtained by conversation (35.3) in Biber's (1988) study. Table 4.2 also reveals a large difference in the standard deviation values (9.1 for conversation and 4.3 for *Friends*), indicating that *Friends* presents much less variation than conversation. This difference can be attributed to the wider range of situations and settings (as described in Chapter 3), ages (from youngsters to octogenarians), and dialectal varieties which were 'captured' by the conversation corpus.

Table 4.2 Descriptive statistics for *Friends* and face-to-face conversation on Biber's D1

Dimension	Register	Mean	Min Value	Max Value	Range	St Dev
D1	*Friends*	<u>34.4</u>	23.7	45.8	22	4.3
	F-T-F Conv	<u>35.3</u>	17.7	54.1	36.4	9.1

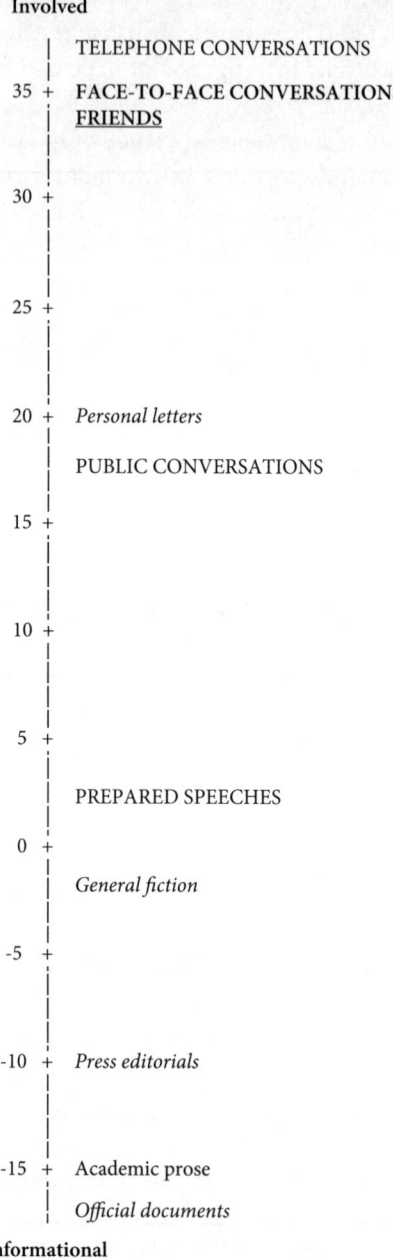

Involved

	|	TELEPHONE CONVERSATIONS
35	+	**FACE-TO-FACE CONVERSATIONS**
	|	<u>**FRIENDS**</u>
	|	
30	+	
	|	
25	+	
	|	
20	+	*Personal letters*
	|	PUBLIC CONVERSATIONS
15	+	
	|	
10	+	
	|	
5	+	
	|	PREPARED SPEECHES
0	+	
	|	*General fiction*
-5	+	
	|	
-10	+	*Press editorials*
	|	
-15	+	Academic prose
	|	*Official documents*

Informational

Figure 4.3 Mean scores of English Dimension 1 for 10 registers, including *Friends*: "Involved versus informational production" (F= 111.9, p <.0001, r^2 = 84.3 percent; spoken registers in small capitals, written registers italicized) (Adapted from Biber, Conrad, & Reppen (1998) to include *Friends*)

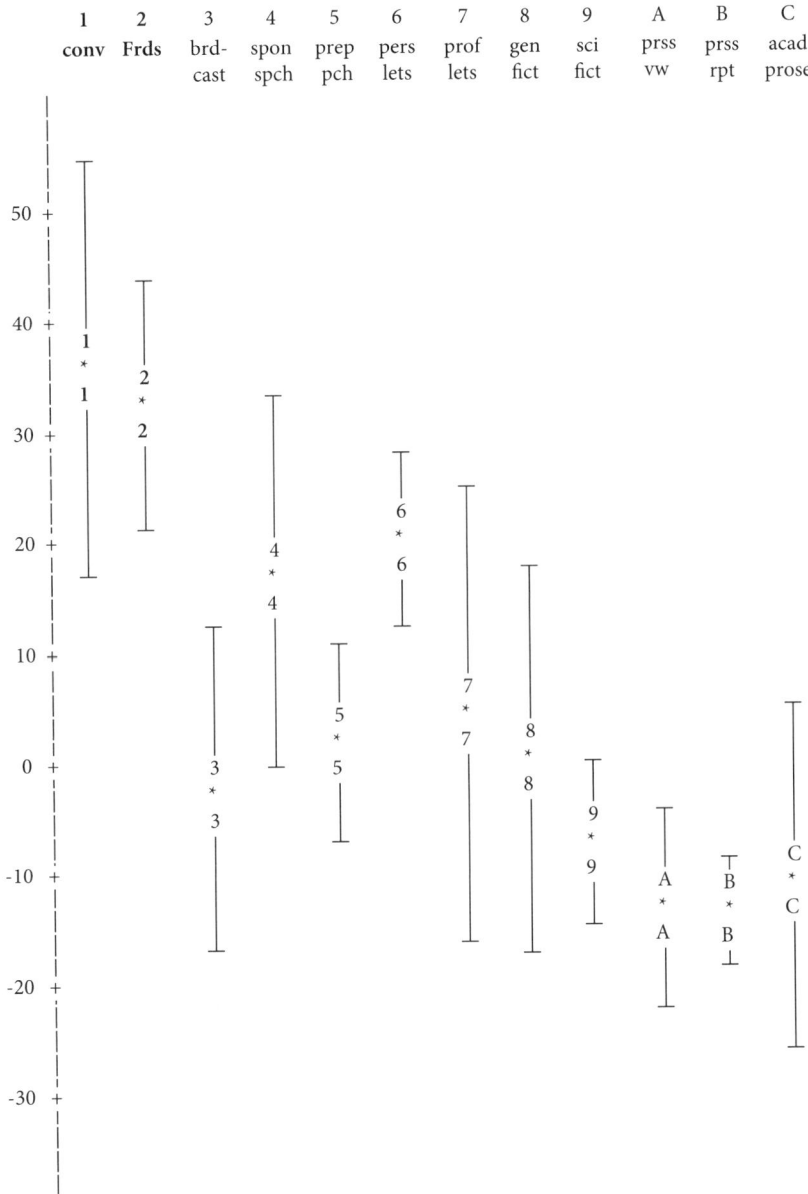

(**Key:** conv = *face-to-face conversation*; Frds = *Friends*; brdcast = *broadcasts*; spon spch = *spontaneous speeches*; prep spch = *prepared speeches*; pers lets = *personal letters*; prof lets = *professional letters*; gen fict = *general fiction*; sci fict = *science fiction*; prss rpt = *press reportage*; prss rvw = *press reviews*; acad prose = *academic prose*)

Figure 4.4 Spread of scores along Dimension 1 ("Involved versus informational production") for 12 registers, including *Friends* (* marks the mean score of each genre) (Adapted from Biber (1988) to include *Friends*)

There is virtually no age variability among the characters in *Friends*. In addition, the language used by the characters is expected to be understood by a wide audience. As such, dialectal differences are probably avoided for the sake of comprehension. In spite of this difference, the analysis shows that the language of *Friends* is characterized by the core linguistic features that typify conversation but without the natural variation that a more comprehensive corpus (as the *Longman Corpus*) is likely to present. Figure 4.3 shows a graphic representation of where *Friends* plotted on D1 along with other selected registers. Figure 4.4 displays the spread of scores on D1, graphically revealing the much smaller variation found in *Friends*.

Therefore, the score obtained by *Friends* on D1 indicates that the language of the television show is similar to face-to-face conversation from a grammatical point of view. In other words, the co-occurrence patterns of linguistic features in *Friends* are similar to those typifying face-to-face conversation and are illustrated in the excerpt below, also shown at the beginning of this chapter.

> Rachel: Hey... Hi you guys! Listen, you know what? I'm not feeling really well. I think I can't get out for the play.
> Ross: Really? Wh-what's wrong?
> Rachel: I don't know! I think it's kind of serious! Oh, you know... I was watching this thing on TV this morning about... Newcastle disease... and I think I might have it!!
> Charlie: Oh, Newcastle disease is a secretion borne virus that only affects chickens and... other poultry.
> Rachel: ...Ok, who is this?
> Ross: I'm sorry, Rachel, this is Charlie Wealer, she's a colleague.
> Rachel: Oh, hi! I would shake your hand but... I'm sure you don't want to get my chicken disease!
>
> [*Friends* – Season 9, episode 20: The One With The Soap Opera Party]

Similarly to conversation, this excerpt from the ninth season of *Friends* has several of the features of Biber's D1. Among other features, it has 11 first-person pronouns (*I*), five second-person pronouns (*you*), nine instances of contractions (e.g., *can't, what's, don't*), 16 examples of present tense verbs (e.g., *think, is, affects*), six private verbs (*feel, think* (three), *know, want*), one hedge (*kind of*), two demonstrative pronouns (*this*), and four discourse particles (*oh* (three), *OK*). The co-occurrence of these features is a reflection of shared context, pressures of real-time production, and the interactive nature of involved registers.

4.5 Summary

In this chapter, I presented the underlying principles of Biber's MD analysis of register variation and outlined the steps taken in his 1988 study. Applying Biber's model of register variation, I compared *Friends* to face-to-face conversation. Results revealed striking similarities between the two corpora on Biber's D1 (involved versus informational production), showing that the language of *Friends* shares the core linguistic features that typify natural conversation.

The two dialogue excerpts that opened this chapter, typical of each of the corpora, present several of the linguistic features of Biber's D1 and are thus illustrative of the similarities between the two registers. The high frequency and co-occurrence of features such as private verbs, first- and second-person pronouns, present tense verbs, contractions, and hedges reflect the interactive nature of conversation and of *Friends*.

In this chapter, I reported the results of the first part of the present study: the MD analysis of *Friends* and the comparison between *Friends* and natural conversation on Biber's D1. As reflected by the results of the analysis, this chapter turned out to be about the similarities between the two corpora. It should be noted, however, that I am not suggesting that *Friends* is the same as conversation. The disparity in the standard deviation shown in the descriptive statistics (4.3 for *Friends* and 9.1 for conversation) indicates that *Friends* presents much less variation than conversation and this should not be overlooked. This difference is probably due to the restricted range of situations, age groups, and dialectal varieties which make up the *Friends* corpus. In Chapters 5–8, I present the second part of the study and focus on functional differences.

CHAPTER 5

Some you know I mean it's really urgh

Vague language

A:	... because they would be hearing voices that would tell them you know to do some weird thing <nv_laugh>
B:	Uh huh
A:	Some you know I mean it's really urgh
B:	<nv_laugh>
A:	<nv_laugh>
B:	Like isn't paranoia kind of like you know schizophrenia
A:	Well it is yeah see that's the thing
B:	Uh huh it's not like a full blown schizophrenia
A:	No well see what they say she has
B:	It's like tendencies

(*Conversation – Longman Grammar Corpus*)

Chandler:	It's alright. Is she good-looking?
Joey:	Yeah, she's totally good looking. I mean, if I met her in a bar, or something, I'd be buying her breakfast…You know, after having slept with her.
Chandler:	Y'know, maybe this isn't such a big deal. Y'know, I mean, the way that I see it is you get a great job and you get to have sex. Y'know, I mean, throw in a tree and a fat guy and you've got Christmas.

(*Friends – Season 2, Episode 10: The One With Russ*)

5.1 Introduction

As reported in the previous chapter, the multidimensional (MD) analysis (Biber, 1988) of *Friends* revealed striking similarities between the television show and conversation on Biber's dimension 1 (involved versus informational production). The results showed that *Friends* shares the core linguistic features that characterize interactive registers, such as face-to-face conversation. Despite the high frequency of most of the linguistic features included in the present study (see Appendix), a closer analysis indicated that groups of features sharing similar discourse functions tended to have higher frequencies in one of the corpora.

The two dialogue excerpts at the beginning of this chapter illustrate the use of one of these groups of features. Conversational hedges such as *kind of like* and *like* (It's _like_[1] tendencies), the discourse markers *you know* and *I mean*, and the noun of vague reference *thing* in the conversation excerpt, and the vague coordination tag *or something* and the stance marker *maybe* in the *Friends* dialogue are some of the linguistic features associated with the typical imprecision and vagueness of conversation. These linguistic features are the object of analysis of this chapter.

5.2 The linguistic expression of vagueness

Vague language is often stigmatized because of the apparent imprecision and ambiguity it brings to conversational exchanges (Overstreet & Yule, 1997) and the potential lack of fluency it may reflect. The use of vague expressions, however, has been shown to be extremely functional in conversation. For example, Carter and McCarthy (2006) state that vague expressions can mitigate the impact that overly direct statements can produce and are also strong indicators of shared knowledge and in-group membership.

The importance of vague language in conversation is attested by the extensive existing literature on this topic. The book-length treatment offered by Channell (1994) is by far the most comprehensive study of vague language to date. Recently, the volume edited by Cutting (2007), *Vague Language Explored*, brings together an impressive collection of articles focusing on different aspects of vague language and contexts in which it is used. However, as Cotterill in Cutting's volume notes, "there is relatively little terminological consensus on vagueness" (p. 98). For example, hedges (e.g., *kind of*) have been labeled *adaptors* (Prince, Bosk, & Frader, 1982), *downtoners* (Jucker, Smith, & Lüdge, 2003), and *fuzziness indicators/approximators* (Wang, 2005). Vague expressions such as *or something* have been called *extension particles* (DuBois, 1993), *vague category markers* (Channell, 1994; Evison, McCarthy, & O'Keefe, 2007), *general extenders* (Overstreet & Yule, 1997), and *coordination tags* (LGSWE). For the most part, I use the terminology utilized in LGSWE and refer the reader to other 'labels' when pertinent.

Vagueness is linguistically realized not only by hedges and vague coordination tags; it is reflected in the use of several other linguistic features, such as nouns of

---

1.   As explained in Chapter 3 (Section 3.8), for practical reasons *like* as a vague device or as a filler was not included in the quantitative analysis.

Table 5.1 Features associated with vague language

Categories	Feature	Conversation	*Friends*	Similar
Hedges	Kind of (like)	•		
	Sort of (like)	•		
Vague coordination tags	Or something (like that)	•		
	Or anything (like that)	•		
	(and) stuff (like that)	•		
Nouns of vague reference	Thing(s)	•		
	Stuff	•		
	Shit	•		
Discourse markers	You know	•		
	I mean			•
Stance markers	Probably	•		
	Perhaps		•	
	Maybe		•	
Modals	Could			•
	Might	•		
Copular verbs	Seem			•
	Appear			•
Utterance final *so*	So	•		

vague reference (e.g., *thing*), some discourse markers (e.g., *you know*), and even some copular verbs (e.g., *seem*). Table 5.1 shows that out of the 18 features associated with vague language chosen for analysis, 10 had higher frequencies in conversation, four had similar counts, and only two of them were more frequent in *Friends*.

Even though I analyze and illustrate the use of these features with examples from both *Friends* and conversation, much of this chapter is about conversation, which, as the frequency counts attest, is much 'more vague' than *Friends*. However, it should be noted that all of these features (with the exception of the taboo word *shit* used as a noun of vague reference) are found in *Friends*. That is to say, *Friends* also has its 'vague moments', but, for reasons to which I will refer later in this chapter, to a much lesser extent when compared to natural conversation. In the following sections, I comment on and exemplify each of these 'vague devices'.

5.2.1 Hedges, vague coordination tags, and nouns of vague reference

Hedges (e.g., *sort of, kind of*), nouns of vague reference (e.g., *stuff, thing*), and vague coordination tags (e.g., *and stuff like that*) are probably the most obvious markers of vagueness in conversation. Figure 5.1 below groups these features together showing that each of these groups of features is more frequent in conversation and that the overall count of these vague devices (6191 times/million words in conversation and 4225 times/million words in *Friends*) is almost 1.5 times more frequent in conversation.

Vague expressions in general and hedges in particular are not used randomly; rather, "they are deliberately chosen for their contribution to the communicative message" (Channell, 1994, p. 197). The apparent imprecision caused by hedges has, in fact, important discourse functions. As Leech (2000) puts it, hedging expressions "allow [ ] a speaker to take refuge in strategic imprecision" (p. 695).

(1) A: and, uh, he showed them to some university professors at UNM or someone did and now <unclear> he's got some <u>sort of</u> honorary degree.
     B: I think they, they gave him permission to go fossil hunting in places where only university folks can go. (Conversation)

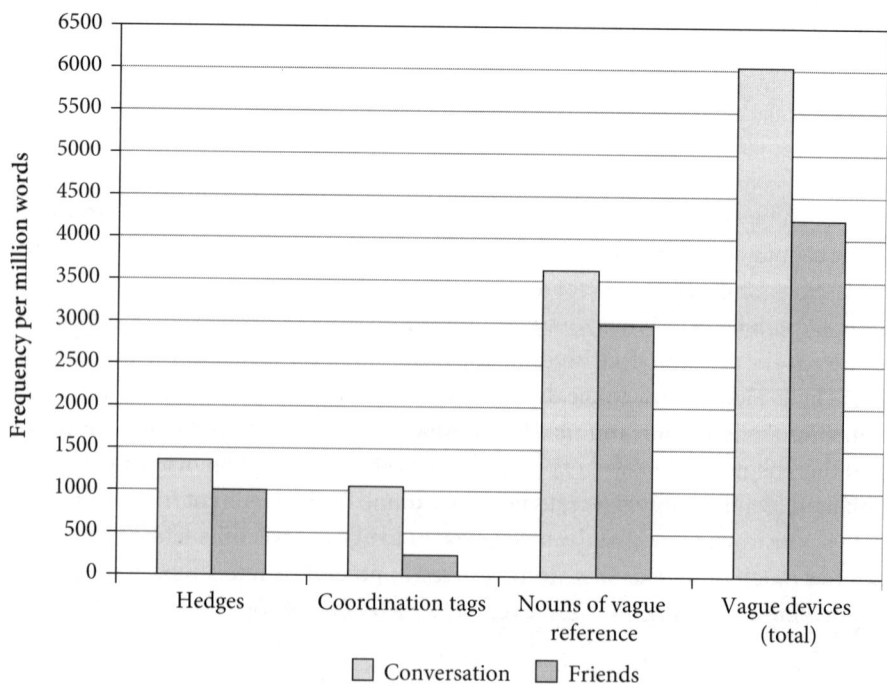

Figure 5.1 Frequency of hedges, coordination tags, and nouns of vague reference

(2) Monica: I hate men! I hate men!
     Phoebe: Oh no, don't hate, you don't want to put that out into the universe.
     Monica: Is it me? Is it like I have some <u>sort of</u> beacon that only dogs and men with severe emotional problems can hear? (*Friends*)

In (1), speaker A is aware that *honorary degree* is not a precise term to describe the referent. In general, the hedge *sort of* is an acknowledgment of this lack of precision and an 'invitation' for the interlocutor to collaboratively construct the intended meaning. Channell (1994) states that this conversational strategy reflects a case of what she calls *lexical gap*, as she explains that "speakers sometimes make use of vagueness to convey meaning in situations where they do not have at their disposal the necessary words or phrases for the concepts they wish to express" (p. 180). The vagueness created by hedges "enables speakers to refer to semantic categories in an open-ended way that calls on shared knowledge to fill in category members referred to obliquely" (McCarthy, 2004, Vagueness and Approximation). In other words, hedges "make it easier for the listener to pick out the specific referent the speaker has in mind if the linguistic expression is not exact" (Aijmer, 1984, p. 122). In fact, they contribute to the creation of a desirable sense of vagueness, as these linguistic devices may lead interlocutors to actively participate in the interaction by asking clarification questions and volunteering possible interpretations. This imprecision ultimately facilitates the interaction between speakers, contributing to the dynamic nature of verbal exchanges.

At first glance, *some sort of beacon* in (2) seems to accomplish the same effect in *Friends*. Notice, however, that Monica does not seem to be 'at a loss for words,' thus not characterizing the lexical gap case that Channel (1994) describes. Obviously meant to create humor, the character elaborates on the creative 'beacon metaphor' in such detail that the combination of the hedged expression and the explanation that follows it winds up having almost the opposite effect that the same *sort of* has in the conversation dialogue. In conversation, the lack of precision brought about by the hedge adds to the dynamic of the exchange as it calls for the participation of the interlocutor; in *Friends*, the addition of humor with the vivid description that follows the hedged expression (that only dogs and men with severe emotional problems can hear?) leaves no room for the interlocutor's participation. And that is when we notice that the *scripted* language of *Friends* differs from conversation. Interestingly, it was the addition of humor that 'disrupted' the naturalness of the exchange.

(3) A: Presto Pasta it's a fast food pasta place.
     B: Pasta's <u>kinda</u> heavy though. (Conversation)

> (4) Phoebe: Please, I almost fell for that with, uh, Pride of the Yankees, I thought I was gonna see a film about Yankee pride and then, boom, the guy gets Lou Gehrig's disease.
>
> Richard: Uh, the guy was Lou Gehrig. Didn't you <u>kinda</u> see it coming? (*Friends*)

Hedges also have another important function. McCarthy and Carter (1997) suggest that the undesirable effect that overly direct utterances can create is functionally mitigated by the imprecision brought about by the use of hedges. In (3) the hedge *kinda* is instrumental in speaker B's expression of non-confrontational disagreement. In *Pasta's <u>kinda</u> heavy though,* this softening effect is enhanced by the use of the adverbial *though* at the end of the utterance. When used in final position in conversation, "*though* makes the disagreement much softer than a marker of direct contrast, such as *but* or *however*" (Biber, Conrad, & Leech, 2002, p. 394). Similarly, in (4), *kinda* in *Didn't you <u>kinda</u> see it coming?* softens the effect that something like "How could you be so stupid?" would have.

> (5) A: If you want to check out that shrine on Sunday <u>or something</u>
>
> B: Yeah, that would be cool. (Conversation)

> (6) Richard: So, you wanna get a hamburger <u>or something</u>?
>
> Monica: Oh, um, I don't know if that's a good idea.
>
> Richard: Oh. Look, just friends, I won't grope you. I promise. (*Friends*)

> (7) A: Well, I'm gonna try to go work out <u>and stuff</u>... <unclear> wants me to get a membership at Gold's.
>
> B: Well, we'll talk about that, I mean, I mean there's a possibility of doing that (Conversation)

> (8) Monica: Or, it could mean that-that you saw Chandler and me together and we y'know were being close <u>and stuff</u> and then you just want to have that with someone too.
>
> Joey: In the dream I did enjoy the closeness. (*Friends*)

The same mitigating effect is achieved in (5) and (6): the vague coordination tag *or something* suggests flexibility and politeness: the speakers' suggestions (i.e., *check out that shrine* and get *a hamburger*) are not set in stone or being imposed on their interlocutors. Indirectly, this open-endedness calls for a negotiation between speakers, thus potentially contributing to the interactiveness of the exchange. The tag *and stuff* in (7) and (8) simplifies the whole statement and "represents an appeal to the listener to construct a referential category" (Overstreet & Yule, 1997, p. 253). Further, this simplification addresses the requirements of face-to-face conversation as it speeds up the communicative process by reducing the potential length of the turn.

Perhaps more important than their soothing effect and their potential contribution to the dynamic of the conversation is the assumption of shared knowledge and informality they bring to the exchanges. As Overstreet and Yule (1997) put it, in American English these vague expressions (*general extenders*, as they call them) seem "to have become primarily … marker[s] of invited solidarity, an indication that the speaker is treating the interlocutor as one who shares (or is willing to act as if they share) the same background knowledge or experience" (p. 256). This assumption of shared knowledge in turn suggests closeness, conveys a sense of informality, and signals an attempt to build interpersonal rapport.

(9) A: Where'd she learn how to do that <u>stuff</u>?
     B: Well, she likes that kind of food… (Conversation)

(10) Ross: You were saying you didn't want to seem stupid.
     Joey: Right, right, right, well, she wants to go to all these cultural places and I don't know how to talk about that <u>stuff</u>. You gotta help me out! (*Friends*)

(11) A: We need silverware.
     B: Um, forks, what is this <u>thing</u>? (Conversation)

(12) Chandler: So uh, what's this <u>thing</u> you're auditioning for?
     Joey: Oh, it's a new TV show… (*Friends*)

(13) A: Well, okay, it's silly to do it now but maybe when I get back I can just load all that <u>shit</u> into my computer. (Conversation)

The use of nouns of vague reference, such as *stuff* in (9) and (10) and *thing* in (11) and (12) result from the pressures of on-line production. If the speakers were to be more precise, they would have to either resort to longer explanations or, perhaps, even interrupt their utterances to think about more precise terms to use. The communicative process is thus expedited through the strategic use of these nouns of vague reference. The taboo word *shit* is not always associated with vague language. In the conversation corpus, it occurs 159 times/million words (out of a total of 244 times/million words) as a noun of vague reference without any apparent derogatory connotation or insulting purpose, as in (13). In this context, *shit* shares the same discourse functions as *thing(s)*. Obviously due to restrictions imposed by NBC (the television network), *shit* is not used in *Friends*.

What is the effect of vague reference in *Friends*? Just like the simplification brought about by the use of vague reference may shorten the length of individual turns, it may also require prolonged exchanges (more air time) due to the need for clarification. In other words, even though vague reference adds to and reflects the interactive nature of conversation, it may not be desirable in television dialogue. These linguistic devices, therefore, have to be well planned and used sparingly in *Friends*. The 'overuse' of vague reference (which would probably correspond to its actual use in natural conversation) may have two undesirable effects: on the one hand, it may require the need for overly extended dialogues; on the other hand, it may result in lack of comprehensibility on the part of the audience, who, in a commercial sense, are actually much more than *virtual* interlocutors of the characters. In other words, the shared context of conversation, which explains much of the use of vague reference, is not likely to be as 'shared' by the actual "intended recipients" (Rühlemann, 2007, p. 14) in *Friends*.

An interesting situation occurs with television dialogue as scriptwriters and actors attempt to produce natural language. As Carter and McCarthy (2006) assert, vagueness "is an important feature of interpersonal meaning and is especially common in everyday conversation" (p. 202). Naturalness in conversation is achieved in part by the frequent use of vague language because the referent is expected to be easily identified by interlocutors. However, as Evison et al. (2007) explain in their analysis of vague category markers (e.g., *stuff like that, or something*), there are different levels of shared context: local, societal, and global.

> 'Local' is defined as interpretable by a specific group of participants and those who share relatively exclusive social and cultural frames of knowledge, for example, a family, a group of friends… 'Societal' is defined as interpretable by all members of a speech community or socio-political entity who share a common culture and history, for instance, English speakers, the population of Ireland, people from a particular city or region. 'Global' is defined as interpretable by most mature, experienced human beings throughout the world. (p. 149)

In their attempt to 'sound natural,' scriptwriters and actors need to keep in mind these levels of shared knowledge. Since *Friends* is about a group of very close friends, a predominantly *local* domain of shared knowledge would be expected. However, the virtual interlocutors (the audience) are characterized by a wide range of socio-cultural backgrounds. In this sense then for the language of the show to be easily understood (and the vagueness easily interpretable), the level of vagueness should be as 'global' as possible, which is likely to compromise the naturalness of the dialogues.

Even though the devices of vague reference discussed thus far are probably the most obvious linguistic markers of vague language, Table 5.1, above, includes other linguistic features which can also contribute to and reflect vagueness: the discourse markers *you know* and *I mean*, the stance markers *probably, perhaps*, and *maybe*, the modal verbs *could* and *might*, the copular verbs *seem* and *appear*, and utterance final *so*. The frequencies of most of these features are shown in Figure 5.2.

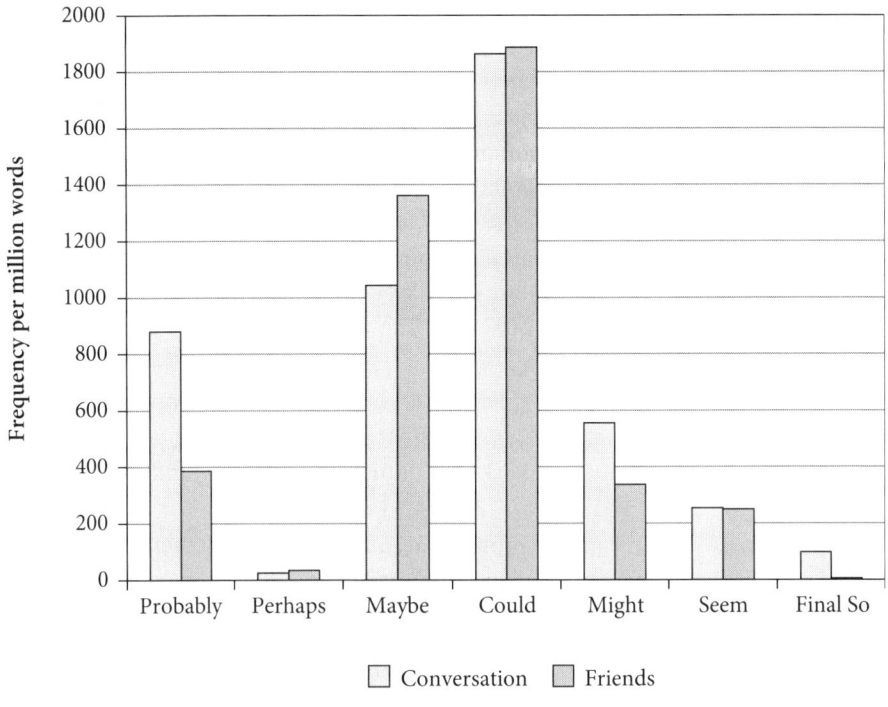

Figure 5.2 Additional features associated with vague language

5.2.2 Discourse markers *you know* and *I mean*

Before discussing *you know* and *I mean*, it is necessary to define 'discourse markers', which is not an easy task. Different authors have referred to items such as *you know*, *I mean*, *okay*, and *right* as *pragmatic expressions* (Erman, 1986), *discourse markers* (e.g., Carter & McCarthy, 2006; Fuller 2003; *Schiffrin, 1987*), *inserts*[2] (LG-SWE), *pragmatic markers* (e.g., Andersen, 2000), and *discourse particles* (Aijmer, 2002). Overall, there seems to be an agreement that this feature has multiple functions (depending on the context), is syntactically optional in the sense that its absence does not change the original proposition (which does *not* mean it does not have important discourse functions), and functions as a cohesive element, signaling

---

2.   LGSWE refers to *inserts* as a category of word (along with lexical words and function words) and explains that "[t]hey do not form an integral part of a syntactic structure, but are inserted rather freely in the text" (p. 56). The authors subdivide this category into different classes, such as interjections (e.g., *oh dear!)*, greetings (e.g., *hi*), discourse markers (e.g., *well*), and hesitators (e.g., *erm*) (pp. 93–94). For detailed descriptions, examples, and analyses of these and many other linguistic features typical of conversation, see Chapter 14 of LGSWE).

relationships between segments of discourse as well as between speakers and hearers.

The authors in LGSWE state that "[t]he items included as 'discourse markers' are open to debate" (p. 1086). They consider discourse markers the "interactive uses" of items such as *well, right, I mean, you know,* and *I see.* According to the authors, discourse markers have two interconnected functions: "a) to signal a transition in the evolving progress of the conversation, and b) to signal an interactive relationship between speaker, hearer, and message" (ibid., p. 1086). For Jucker and Smith (1998), discourse markers "are one type of cue that conversationalists use to negotiate their common ground" (p. 172). The authors classify discourse markers into two major categories: *reception markers* and *presentation markers.* For the authors, the former "are used to signal a reaction to information provided by another speaker" (p. 174) and include items such as *yeah, oh,* and *okay*; the latter "accompany and modify the speaker's own information" (p. 174) and include items such as *like, you know,* and *I mean.*[3]

Carter and McCarthy (2006) provide a useful summary that seems to incorporate elements that are agreed upon by most researchers:

> Discourse markers function to organise and monitor an ongoing discourse, most commonly in speech, by marking boundaries between one topic and the next (so, right), by indicating openings (well, right) and closure and pre-closure (okay) of topics, by indicating topic changes (well) or by bringing a conclusion to the discourse (anyway, so). They also function to mark the state of knowledge between participants (you know, you see, I mean). (p. 901)

As I indicated in Chapter 1, Section 1.2, engaging in a discussion of the terminology ascribed to whatever linguistic features is beyond the scope of this project. For the purposes of this study, I use the term *discourse marker* to identify what Jucker and Smith (1998) categorized as presentation markers (e.g., *you know, I mean, well*); I then refer to Jucker and Smith's (ibid.) conceptualization of reception markers as 'non-minimal responses' (McCarthy, 2002), when addressing single-word responses (see Chapter 6 on emotional language and Chapter 8 on narrative language).

The discourse marker *you know* (not included in the chart so as not to dwarf the other frequency bars) is 3 times more frequent in conversation: it occurs 4990 times/million words in conversation and 1563 times/million words in *Friends.* Aijmer (1984) suggests that because *you know* often collocates with *kind of* and *sort of,* it shares the same function, thus contributing to the vague nature of conversation, as in (14) and (15). Overstreet and Yule (1997) also observe that often this co-occurrence "represent[s] points in …interactions where one speaker indicates

---

3.   The authors subdivide presentation markers into two subcategories: information-centered (e.g., *like*) and addressee-centered (e.g., *you know, I mean*).

an expectation that the other will be able to complete the message" (p. 225), which seems to be the case especially in (14).

(14)   … you could just <u>sort of</u> open them up yeah and just <u>you know</u> <u>kind of</u> spread them out … (Conversation)

(15)   Chandler: Those were like the best seats ever.
         Joey: Oh yeah. Hey! Should we give these shirts to the girls? <u>Y'know</u>, <u>kinda like</u> a peace offering. (*Friends*)

Compared to *you know*, *I mean* (also not included in the chart) is less frequent in both *Friends* and conversation and has similar counts in both corpora (2343 times/ million words in *Friends* and 2303 times/million words in conversation). In (16), similar to a pause or a hesitator, *I mean* seems to function as a filler, co-occurring with two instances of the hesitator *uh*; in (17), as Rachel admits that she thought Chandler was gay when she first met him, *I mean* seems to have the same filler function, co-occurring with the hesitator *uh* at the beginning of the utterance and several devices associated with vague language: the discourse marker *you know*, the stance markers *maybe* and *possibly*, and the modal *might*. The combination of these devices further soothes the impact that a direct statement (e.g., *Yes, I thought you were gay.*) would have. In addition, notice that even the word *gay* is elided in Rachel's utterance, highlighting the sensitivity of the topic.

(16)   A.   I don't, I don't know <nv_laugh> yeah if you guys want to that'd be great.
         B.   He's, he's doing a project in which taping conversation just <u>uh</u> you know <u>I mean uh</u>, well how do you put it
         C.   Collecting data. (Conversation)

(17)   Rachel: <u>Uh</u>… yeah. Well, <u>I mean</u>, when I first met you, <u>y'know</u>, I thought <u>maybe</u>, <u>possibly</u>, you <u>might</u> be…
         Chandler: You did? (*Friends*)

In addition to the filler function, *I mean* is much more often used as a 'clarification device'. According to Schiffrin (1987), "*I mean* marks a speaker's upcoming modification of the meaning of his/her own prior talk" (p. 296). More specifically, "*I mean* signals that a clarification is going to follow" (LGSWE, p. 1077), thus indicating the speaker's awareness of the vagueness of his/her own utterance. In this sense, *I mean* does not contribute to the vagueness of the utterance; rather it *reflects* the vagueness of the chunk of utterance preceding it.

(18)   …I think they miss the point because in, in the winter ceremonial when they pretend to cut off somebody's, <u>you know</u>, and do all this other <u>kind of</u> stuff, it's the show, <u>I mean</u>, they know this is true and, <u>you know</u>, the near-

er you can make it look like it's true, the better job you're doing, uh...
(Conversation)

(19)   Monica: This woman's got my life, I should get to see who she is.
       Rachel: Go to the post office! I'm sure her picture's up!...Okay, Monica,
                 y'know what, honey, you're <u>kinda</u> losing it here! <u>I mean</u>, this is
                 really becoming <u>like</u> a weird obsession <u>thing</u>. (*Friends*)

In (18), *I mean* clearly indicates the upcoming clarification and co-occurs with *you know* and *kind of*. The same function of *I mean* is illustrated in (19), where the need for clarification resulted from the preceding use of the hedge *kinda*. *You're kinda losing it here!* is 'translated' as *a weird obsession thing*, with the addition of the hedge *like* used to mitigate the impact of the statement, and the noun of vague reference *thing*, used in lieu of a more precise term. Interestingly, this particular exchange was clearly not meant to be humorous. This time, the lack of the humor element resulted in a more natural exchange, more similar to natural conversation.

Whether clarifying the previous chunk of utterance or reflecting vagueness, the frequent co-occurrence of these features (*you know, I mean, sort of, kind of, like*) suggests that they share similar discourse functions. Also reflecting vagueness, the stance markers *probably, perhaps*, and *maybe* are analyzed in the next section.

5.2.3   Stance markers *probably*, *perhaps*, and *maybe*

Conrad and Biber (2000) refer to stance as "a cover term for the expression of personal feelings and assessment in three major domains: epistemic stance,...attitudinal stance, ...and style stance" (p. 57). In this study, I focus exclusively on epistemic stance, which "can mark certainty (or doubt), actuality, precision, or limitation..." (LGSWE, p. 972). Examples of this category of stance markers are *possibly* (doubt), *actually* (actuality), *sort of* ((im)precision), and *generally* (limitation).

The stance markers discussed in this section add one more element to the 'vague picture': uncertainty or lack of commitment. *Probably* is described in LGSWE as one of the most frequent stance adverbials in conversation expressing doubt and uncertainty. It is almost over twice more frequent in conversation, occurring 880 times/million words. Carter (2003) refers to adverbs such as *probably* and *possibly* as *modal expressions* as they "play a part in making sure...that utterances don't sound too assertive or definite. Like 'vague language,' these modal expressions help to soften what is said" (p. 11). The 'doubt component' of these adverbials often achieves this mitigating effect.

Similar to *probably*, the stance markers *maybe* and *perhaps* are used to express uncertainty. *Perhaps* is much less frequent than *maybe* in American English conversation, occurring 26 times/million words; in *Friends*, it occurs 35 times/million words. *Maybe* occurs 1044 times/million words in conversation and 1361 times/ million in *Friends*. Excerpt (20) shows the co-construction of doubt and uncertainty by two different speakers. The sensitive topic (AIDS) leads speaker A to resort to the use of the hedge *like* in an attempt to mitigate the difficulty or perhaps sadness of addressing the issue. With *probably*, speaker B adds to the atmosphere of uncertainty; speaker A keeps the uncertain tone of the discussion combining *maybe* with the vague coordination tag *or something*.

(20) A. They just said he had AIDS, <u>like</u> full blown, it wasn't <u>like</u> stages, it was <u>like</u> he just had
     B. He <u>probably</u> never got, never went to the hospital.
     A. <u>Maybe</u> he was in denial <u>or something</u>.
     B. Yeah. (Conversation)

In (21), *maybe* co-occurs with the hedge *like* and the vague coordination tag *or something*, and is used to suggest or invite. It is interesting to notice how the stance marker and the two conversational hedges complement one another to make the suggestion less direct, in a clear attempt to not impose on the interlocutor. Finally, in (22), the speakers are discussing what *might have happened* in their lives had they made different decisions: the first speaker uses the modal *might* (see next section) to convey uncertainty; this uncertainty is maintained by the second speaker with the stance marker *perhaps*. Like in (20), it is interesting to observe this co-construction of mood or tone of the interactions.

(21) Phoebe: <u>Maybe</u> we can <u>like</u> go to a movie <u>or something</u>.
     Ross: Okay. (*Friends*)

(22) Phoebe: Yeah, I <u>might</u> have said yes, but that would have been wrong.
     David: Please, you don't have to explain. I mean, <u>perhaps</u> if I hadn't gone to Minsk things would have worked out for us. (*Friends*)

5.2.4 Modal verbs *might* and *could*

Just like the stance markers analyzed in the previous section, the modals *might* and *could* are used to express possibility and often convey doubt or uncertainty. They often co-occur with "modality expressions" (Carter, 2003) such as *probably* and *maybe*, an indication that they share similar discourse functions. *Might* occurs 398 times/million words in *Friends* and 581 times/million words in conversation. In (23), it co-occurs with *probably* and *maybe* in the same chunk of discourse. *Might* and *probably* are used to express a logical yet uncertain conclusion, as the same speaker who had used *might* contemplates the possible need to "*give her another fifty for that*" with the stance marker *maybe*.

(23)   A. He's going to send her the Fed Ex account number, yeah.
       B. Okay.
       A. The only thing she <u>might</u> have to pay for is having it put in a box with styrofoam
       B. Yeah, she <u>probably</u> will at one of those mailbox places.
       A. <u>Maybe</u> I should give her another fifty for that. (Conversation)

Could has almost identical counts in conversation (1863 times/million words) and in *Friends* (1886 times/million words). In addition to expressing uncertainty, *could* is also used in indirect requests as part of a polite formula. Example (24) from *Friends* offers an interesting combination of markers of uncertainty and indirect request. *Probably*, *could*, and *like* set the initial tone of the utterance and are followed by *might* and *like*; the combination of *maybe* and *could* is a clear attempt to ensure that the utterance be perceived as a "tentative indirect request" (Aijmer, 1996, p. 140), thus softening the impact that an overly assertive request could have.

(24)   Phoebe: I know! So this woman <u>probably</u> <u>could</u> <u>like</u> have all kinds of stories about my parents, and she <u>might</u> even know <u>like</u> where my Dad is. So I looked her up, and she lives out by the beach. So <u>maybe</u> this weekend we <u>could</u> go to the beach?
       All: Yeah! Yeah, we can! (*Friends*)

In (25), *could* is used to express uncertainty. Notice how speaker A combines a series of markers of vagueness and uncertainty: the discourse markers *I mean* and *you know*, the stance marker *probably*, the modal *could*, the vague coordination tag *and stuff*, and the hedge *like*. In this example, this uncertainty seems to reflect Speaker A's degree of commitment (or lack thereof) – his unwillingness to use his car. As Jucker et al. (2003) show, one of the functions of these vague devices is to indicate the degree of commitment speakers may have toward a proposition. Because of all of this hedging, speaker A's utterances are virtually unintelligible to us as we do not have access to the context shared by the two interlocutors. It is not hard to imagine that this degree of vagueness would not be desirable in *Friends*.

(25)   A: My car <u>I mean</u> it's pretty... <u>you know</u> I don't know if it
       B: <nv_clears throat>
       A: <u>I mean</u> it <u>probably</u> <u>could</u> make it but then tires <u>and stuff</u> too yeah my tires
       B: Do you have to get new tires?
       A: Well <u>probably</u> I haven't <u>like</u> I always forget to <u>like</u> put air in them <nv_laugh> (Conversation)

5.2.5 Copular verbs *seem* and *appear*

"Current copular verbs," such as *seem* and *appear*, "identify attributes that are in a continuing state of existence" and are differentiated from "resulting copular verbs," such as *become*, *get*, and *end up*, which "identify an attribute that happens as a result of some process of change" (LGSWE, p. 436). *Seem* and *appear* provide a hedged interpretation of varied states of existence or appearance. *Seem* is much more common than *appear* in conversational registers, presenting almost identical counts in conversation (254 times/million words) and *Friends* (249 times/million words); *appear* occurs only 5 times/million words in conversation and 7 times/ million words in *Friends*, thus not being productive for analysis. In (26), *seem* is preceded by the hedge *kinda*; in (27), speaker A conveys hedged doubt with *seem* followed by the adjective *improbable*, intensifying the tone of uncertainty, which is corroborated by speaker B with *Yeah, that doesn't sound right*.

> (26) Mona: So it was really cool seeing you lecture today.
> Ross: Oh thanks. Although it <u>kinda</u> <u>seemed</u> like you were falling asleep there a little.
> Mona: Oh no-no, I-I had my eyes closed so I could concentrate and y'know take it all in.
> Ross: Yeah, a lot of my students do that. (*Friends*)
> (27) A: …I mean I asked the guy if it had a new engine put in it 'cause it <u>seemed</u> improbable that being that old that it would only have that many miles on it.
> B: Yeah, that doesn't sound right. (Conversation)

5.2.6 Utterance final *so*

Vagueness can also be created at the discourse level. *So* at the end of turns seems to have this function. In (28), *so* not only indicates that the speaker intends to 'transfer the floor' to the interlocutor; it also has the function of transferring to the interlocutor the responsibility of concluding whatever thought the speaker would have uttered after the self-interrupted *so-* sequence. This interruption adds to the vague atmosphere created by the presence of the noun of vague reference *thing*, two instances of the discourse marker *you know*, and the hedge *kind of like*. By the same token, this device expedites the turn-taking dynamic of the communicative process. This use of *so* thus constitutes a "form of reduction at the discourse level and a clear indication of how speakers perceive the communicative process as interactive and co-constructed" (Quaglio & Biber, 2006, p. 711).

(28) A. Well, the other <u>thing</u> is the garlic that I've had is been released, tons of it, <u>you know</u>, <u>kind of like</u> going to um Colossio, <u>you know</u>. Arrgh. <u>So</u>…

   B. Yeah. (Conversation)

5.3 Summary

Conversation presents a higher frequency of most of the linguistic features discussed in this section, suggesting that it tends to be vaguer than *Friends*. In natural conversation, ideas, propositions, feelings and opinions are rarely elaborated as "greater precision is unnecessary or even harmful because it could hold up the progress of the conversation. Hints and rough indications, relying on shared knowledge, are often just what is needed" (Biber, Conrad, & Leech, 2002, p. 431). Further, in conversation, overly vague utterances can be easily addressed by speakers by means of clarification questions, for example. Vagueness is less desirable in *Friends*, as the audience (the interlocutors of the show) cannot interact with the characters. It appears that the use of vague devices in *Friends* is constrained by a "clarity cut-off boundary," beyond which comprehension can be adversely affected.

I have also tried to show that the differences between *Friends* and conversation go beyond the disparity in frequency counts of vague devices. There is a clear indication that the 'addition' of humor may wind up interfering with the natural flow of the exchanges and the function of these devices. A case in point was illustrated in example (2): in "…*Is it like I have some <u>sort of</u> beacon that only dogs and men with severe emotional problems can hear?*" the simplifying purpose of the hedge *sort of* is defeated by the overly elaborated description of the hedged noun *beacon*, giving us an indication of the potential interference of scripted language in the natural flow of the dialogues in *Friends*.

Finally, another potential difference between conversation and *Friends* relating to the use of vague devices lies in the need for the show to be easily interpretable by a general audience. Using the taxonomy proposed by Evison et al. (2007), the level of knowledge shared by close friends (as is the case in *Friends*) is 'local;' however, for the sake of comprehensibility scriptwriters and actors need to linguistically keep the level of vagueness as close as possible to the 'global' domain.

CHAPTER 6

I am just really really happy...

Emotional language

Rachel:	You <u>really</u> think I didn't say goodbye to you because I don't care?
Ross:	That's what it seemed like.
Rachel:	<u>I cannot believe</u> that after ten years, you do not know ONE thing about me.
Ross:	<u>Fine</u>, then why didn't you say something?
Rachel:	Because it is <u>too</u> <u>damn</u> hard Ross. I can't even begin to explain to you how much I'm gonna miss you.

[*Friends*: Season 10, episode 16 – The One With Rachel's Going Away Party]

A:	She's a phlebotomist...can you believe Denell doing that?
B:	No.
A:	Can you believe Denell <shouting>doing that</shouting>. I mean, I said, every time I see her, Denell <u>I can't believe</u>, oh and she's <u>so</u> good, I mean she's <u>so</u>, her fingers are <u>so</u> tender when she's you know what I mean and she must be, well, now this isn't, Father said there's a difference between bragging and facts.
B:	Okay. (Conversation)

6.1 Introduction

In involved spoken registers, such as casual conversation, participants express feelings, attitudes, and concerns. This involvement is reflected in the speakers' tone of voice, intonation patterns, nonverbal signals, and linguistic features. This chapter focuses on the linguistic choices speakers make to convey their feelings and express stance. I describe these features, compare their frequencies in *Friends* and conversation, and provide examples from both corpora.

I use the cover term *emotional language*[1] to refer to any emphatic form of expression that is captured by the use of certain linguistic features and can be identified in a transcribed corpus and studied from a grammatical standpoint. Consider, for instance, the example below:

> Joey: Oh, hey! Why don't you book a date for both of you at one of those romantic spas?
>
> Phoebe: Ooh Joey, that's actually a <u>really</u> good idea! (*Friends*)

The adverbial intensifier *really*, one of the linguistic markers of emotional language, adds emphasis to Phoebe's utterance. This emphasis can thus be perceived even without access to the audio file containing this exchange or without any prosodic information (e.g., intonation patterns). The two excerpts from *Friends* and conversation that open this chapter have some of the markers of emotional language which are the object of analysis of this chapter: the lexical bundle *I can't believe*, adverbial intensifiers *so* and *really*, and expletive *damn*.

It is true that individual utterances can be emphasized or emotionally-loaded and not contain any of the linguistic markers selected for the purpose of this study. This type of information can be captured only when the corpus is annotated for prosodic features or when it is commented by the transcriber. As pointed out in Chapter 3, one of the versions of the *Friends* corpus contains comments made by the transcribers. For example, in the exchanges below Chandler is mad at Ross for kissing his mother, Mrs. Bing, and mad at Joey for knowing and not telling him about it:

> Chandler: I'm still mad at you for not telling me.
>
> Joey: What are you mad at me for?!
>
> Ross: Chandler–
>
> Chandler: You gotta let me slam the door! (Leaves; slams the door)
>
> Joey: (Shouting after him) Chandler, I didn't kiss her, he did! (To Ross) See what happens when you break the code? (*Friends*)

This short exchange offers clues to the potential emotional content of the utterances by means of the lexical meanings of *mad* and *slam*. The emotional nature of the dialogue is confirmed by the transcriber's comments in parentheses, but was not captured in my analysis. In most situations, however, there is a combination of lexical items (emphatic or emotionally-loaded by virtue of their semantic nature) and linguistic features associated with emotional language. For example, in the segment below the lexical verbs *hate* and *kill* co-occur with the adverbial intensifiers

---

1.   In this study, the differences between emotive (intentional, planned) and emotional (spontaneous) language are not considered. For this discussion, see, for example, Arndt and Janney (1991) and Caffi and Janney (1994).

really and *so* in the same chunk of discourse, reinforcing the emotional nature of the exchanges. This chapter describes and discusses linguistic features such as *really* and *so*.

Rachel: I **hate** this apartment! I **hate** the color of these walls! I **hate** the fact that this place still smells like bird! I **hate** that singing guy!

Joey: Are you kidding? I love that guy! (Starts singing) Morning's here! Morning is here—

Rachel: Stop it! I will **kill** you. I **hate** the fact that my room is _so_ small.

Monica: Hey, I have all the space I need. Just do what I did.

Rachel: Monica, you don't even have a bed, you sleep in a ball on the floor!

Monica: Y'know what? I am _really_ tired of your bellyaching! Okay, I-I worked _really_ hard at making this a nice place for us to live!

Rachel: I'm sorry. I'm _so_ sorry.

As it will become evident in the discussion below, *Friends* turned out to be much more 'emotional' than natural conversation. This difference is reflected in the overuse of most features associated with emotionally-loaded language in *Friends*. However, all linguistic features are found in both corpora (except for the taboo terms *shit* and *fuck* -- found only in conversation), as was the case with the analysis of vague language. If the previous chapter was more about conversation than *Friends*, this chapter is more about *Friends*. As such, even though I provide examples from both corpora, most of them come from *Friends*.

6.2 The linguistic expression of emotion/emphatic content

Several features have been associated with the expression of stance and emphatic content. Among these features are intensifiers (e.g., *so*), discourse markers (e.g., *oh*), non-minimal responses (McCarthy, 2002) (e.g., *wow*), stance markers (e.g., *of course*), expletives/taboo terms (e.g., *damn*), and slang terms (e.g., *cool*). Based on a survey of LGSWE and other scholarly works cited here, 32 features associated with emotional language were chosen for analysis. Table 6.1 shows that 25 of these features were more frequent in *Friends*, three had similar counts, and only four of them were more frequent in conversation.

Table 6.1 Features associated with emotional and/or emphatic content

Category	Feature	Conversation	*Friends*	Similar
Intensifiers	Very			•
	So		•	
	Really		•	
	Too			•
	Totally		•	
	Damn			•
Discourse markers	Oh		•	
	Wow		•	
Stance marker	Of course		•	
Non-minimal responses	Wow	•		
	Sure		•	
	Fine		•	
Expletives	Damn (overall)		•	
	Bastard		•	
	Bitch(y)		•	
	Son of a bitch		•	
	Shit(ty)	•		
	Fuck (and variations)	•		
	Ass (part of expression)		•	
	Crap(py)		•	
Innovations	All + adjective/gerund		•	
	Totally		•	
Lexical Bundles	I can't believe (+ complements)		•	
	Thank you so much		•	
Emphatic *do*	Emphatic *do*		•	
Copular verbs	Look		•	
	Feel		•	
	Sound		•	
Slang terms	Suck		•	
	Piss(ed)(off)	•		
	Screw(ed)(up)		•	
	Freak out		•	

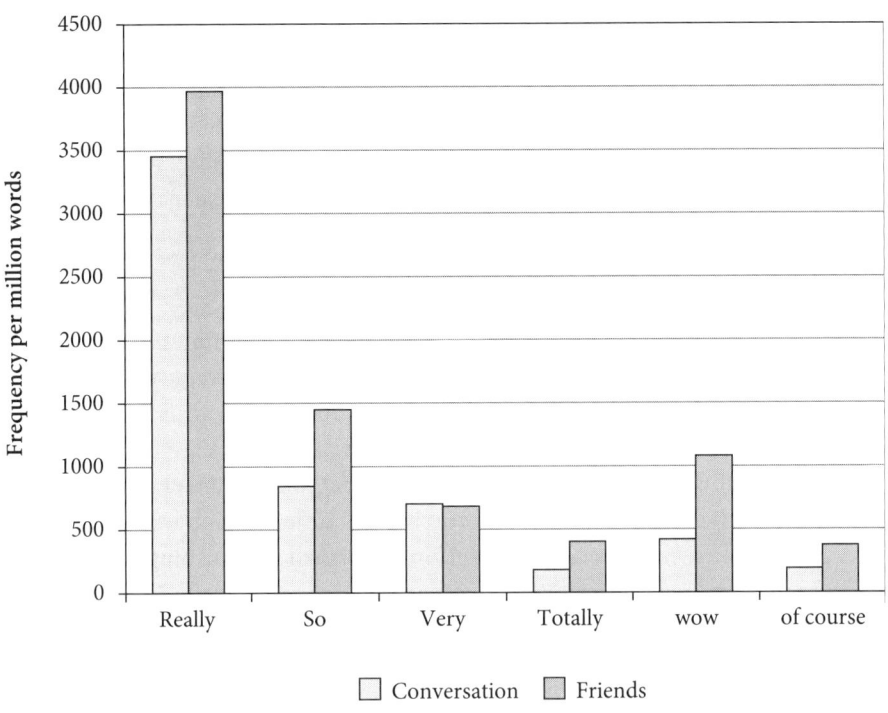

Figure 6.1 Major features associated with emphatic/emotional content

Among the more obvious features indicating emphatic and emotional content are the adverbial intensifiers *very*, *so*, *really*, and *totally*, the discourse markers *oh* and *wow*, and the stance marker *of course*. Figure 6.1 groups these features (except *oh*) and shows that, with the exception of *very*, all of them are more frequent in *Friends*.

6.2.1 Adverbial intensifiers

Adverbial intensifiers (or amplifiers) are "degree adverbs that increase intensity" (LGSWE, p. 554) or, as Tagliamonte and Roberts (2005) put it, "adverbs that boost or maximize meaning" (p. 280). LGSWE (pp. 564–6) reports that adverbial intensifiers are most common in conversation, especially *very*, *so*, *really/real*, *too*, and *totally*[2]. Speakers use a wide range of informal intensifiers to express stance, emotion, and for emphatic purposes. Out of the six intensifiers selected for analysis (*so*, *really*, *totally*, *very*, *too*, *damn*), three were more frequent in *Friends* (*so*, *really*,

---

2. See Tagliamonte and Roberts (2005) for an excellent summary of the history of intensifiers. Also, see their analysis of use of adjectives in *Friends*, including quality of adjectives (emotional, neutral) as well as their distribution by sex.

totally) and three of them had similar counts (*very, too, damn*). As acknowledged in LGSWE (pp. 857–8), the function of the adverb *really* can be ambiguous, especially in medial position, as the characterization of the stance adverbial (meaning *in fact*) and the adverbial intensifier is by no means clear-cut.[3] Since both the intensifying function and the epistemic stance meaning relate to the expression of attitude, all instances of *really* were included in the automatic frequency analysis.[4]

> (1) Rachel: Hello. But you know what, hey, new day, new leaf, I am just re-ally really happy... (*Friends*)

Really occurs 3968 times/million words in *Friends* and 3456 times/million words in conversation. In (1), the repetition of *really* intensifies its amplifying effect. Interestingly, the second most frequent right collocate of *really* in *Friends* is *really*, co-occurring 121 times/million words; in conversation, there are only 38 times/ million words instances of this collocation. The first most frequent right collocate of *really* in both corpora is *good*, co-occurring 129 times/million words in *Friends* and 203/million words in conversation. In a nutshell, when things are *good* in *Friends*, they are not *really good* only; rather, they are *really, really good*!

> (2) Monica: Wait a minute, wait a minute. Yes he is. You are totally differ-ent. (*Friends*)
> (3)   I'm totally gonna do it. (Conversation)
> (4) Joey: I'm telling ya, you guys are totally getting back together! (*Friends*)
> (5) Rachel: I was giving you an apology and you were totally checking her out! (*Friends*)

The word *totally* has become more and more frequent in the past 10 years or so in American English. One of the reasons is that it is being used in innovative ways: in addition to its 'canonical function' in which it is clearly interchangeable with

---

3.   Even though videos of the show were available for disambiguation, analyzing the intonation patterns and/or nonverbal cues attached to every instance of *really* was not feasible due to its very high frequency in both corpora. In addition, this prosodic information was not available for the conversation corpus.

4.   See Carter and McCarthy (2006, pp. 134–135) for a good summary of the functions of *really*. The softening function of *really* (often in negative sentences and in final position, as in "... *it's not that we don't want to, really...*" or in "*No, not really...*" as well as its "concessive meaning of 'despite what has just been said'" (p. 134), as in "*He's got a terrible temper, but he's a lovely guy really.*" (ibid.) account for a very small proportion of the data. In *Friends*, when absolutely not ambiguous, only 46 instances per million words (out of a total of 3968 occurrences per million words) were found with these functions; conversation yielded a very similar count: 49 instances per million words.

completely (with a sense of completeness or totality) as in (2), it is also used as an intensifier (without the completeness connotation) and is interchangeable with *really*, as in (3). *Totally* is also used with the meaning of *for sure* or *definitely (without a doubt)*, as in (4), and is not interchangeable with completely (with its canonical meaning); in (5), it apparently has the meaning of *inconspicuously* or, perhaps, *shamelessly* (in this case) and does not seem to be interchangeable with *completely* from a semantic standpoint either.

Notice that in most of these innovative uses *totally* precedes a verb. The third use, perhaps the most innovative (emphatic agreement), is discussed in Section 6.2.5. As an adverbial intensifier, it is over twice more frequent in *Friends*, occurring 402 times/million words; in conversation, it occurs 180 times/million words with this function. The semantic sense of *totally* is dependent on the speaker's intention, and, at times, one can argue that it could have any of the meanings discussed above. The semantic connotations of *totally* illustrated in (3), (4), and (5) seem to be becoming more and more common in American English conversation. In an informal survey, native speakers of American English (ages between 25 and 40), analyzed the instances of *totally* in both corpora based on this classification. According to them, out of the 402 instances/million words of *totally* in *Friends*, 101 instances/million words had one of these three new meanings; in conversation, these meanings were found 46 times/million words out of the total of 180 times/million words. Interestingly, despite the large difference in frequency, in both corpora these innovations account for 25% of the instances.

Another possible indication of the increasing popularity of *totally* seems to be the expansion of its semantic preference when preceding adjectives. Partington (2004) found a predominant preference for collocates indicating "absence" or "lack of," such as *bald*, *incapable*, and *naked*; she also found a group of collocates indicating "change of state" or "transformation," such as *destroyed*, *different*, and *transformed* (p.147)[5]. In *Friends*, only about 40% of the adjectives collocating with *totally* fit the absence or change of state category. Some of the examples not fitting this category are: *good*, *okay*, *true*, and *rational*. In conversation, a little over 50% of the collocates did not fit the absence or change of state category. *White*, *surprised*, *natural*, and *gorgeous* are some examples.

(6)　　　　　Too <u>damn</u> bad, huh? (Conversation)
(7)　Phoebe:　Well, just buy the <u>damn</u> boat! (*Friends*)
(8)　　　　　Yeah but in a town like Washington where it's <u>damn</u> well close to closing anyway… (Conversation)

5.　It should be noted, however, that Partington's data comprised British academic writing.

(9)   Chandler: Ooh-hoo. <u>Very</u> hot, <u>very</u> sexy. But ah, y'know she's <u>too</u> international, y'know she's never gonna be around. (*Friends*)

Overall, *damn* is almost twice more frequent in *Friends* (190 times/million words vs. 97 times/million words in conversation); for the analysis of adverbial intensifiers, however, only instances in which *damn* modifies an adjective as in (6), a noun as in (7), and an adverbial as in (8) were considered. The frequencies were almost identical in both corpora: 51 times/million words in *Friends* and 49 times/million words in conversation. The intensifier *too*, illustrated in (6) and (9), had very similar counts in *Friends* (249 times/million words) and conversation (256 times/million words). Example (9) also contains two instances of *very*. Like *too*, the frequency of *very* was very similar in both corpora (702 times/million words in conversation and 681 times/million words in *Friends*).

In conclusion, the analysis of adverbial intensifiers reveals that all features are found in both corpora and are used similarly. *Friends*, however, makes use of them more frequently. The co-occurrence of these intensifiers with other emotionally-loaded linguistic features (discussed below) characterizes the more emotional tone of the dialogues in *Friends*.

6.2.2 Discourse markers *oh, wow* and stance marker *of course*

Two of the most frequent discourse markers (see Chapter 5, Section 5.2.2 for the definition of discourse markers) in conversation selected for analysis are associated with the expression of feelings, emotion, or emphatic language: *oh* and *wow*. Numerous functions have been attributed to the discourse marker *oh*, but all of them "express a mental reaction to a stimulus (Aijmer, 1987, p. 61). *Oh*, the most frequent discourse marker in both corpora (not included in Figure 6.1 so as not to dwarf the other features), is 1.6 times more frequent in *Friends*: it occurs 12808 times/million in *Friends* and 7973 times/million in conversation; *wow* is 2.6 times more frequent in *Friends*, occurring 1081 times/million words.

(10) Joey: <u>Wow</u>! You look... stop-eating hot! Which is like the highest
                   level of hotness!
       Phoebe: Are you sure? Because I'm <u>really</u> dreading going to this party.
                   (*Friends*)

(11) Rachel: Yeah, I-I heard. I think it's great! <u>Oh</u>, I'm <u>so</u> happy for you!
       Chandler: <u>Oh</u>, well, that's great! (*Friends*)

(12) Mindy: Will you be my maid of honor?
       Rachel: <u>Of course</u>!
       Mindy: <u>Oh</u> that's <u>so</u> great! (*Friends*)

(13) A: Cause you can see there's a little um, battery thing
      B: Okay.
      A: Little meter that tells you
      B: <u>Wow</u> that <u>really</u> does need a lot of juice.
      A: Oh yeah. See it tells you plus it's got this whole thing happening. See this is where the battery is… (Conversation)

Overall, stance markers are much more frequent in conversation than in any other register (Conrad & Biber, 2000). *Of course* expresses certainty and is twice more frequent in *Friends*, occurring 374 times/million words; the conversation corpus yielded 190 instances per million words. It is interesting to notice how the features associated with emphatic/emotional content tend to co-occur, especially in *Friends*. Perhaps even more interesting is the fact that this co-occurrence is often realized by different speakers, reflecting the collaborative nature of conversation as speakers co-construct the communicative event (LGSWE, Chapter 14). This is obviously the case in conversation, but occurs much more often in *Friends*. In (10), for example, *wow* is used by the first speaker with an exclamatory intent; the second speaker maintains the emotional tone of the exchange by using *really* as an intensifier modifying the verb *dreading*. *So* and *oh* are combined by the first speaker in (11), while the second speaker uses *oh* in an exclamatory utterance. Finally, in (12) the emotional content of the exchange is intensified with the co-occurrence of *of course*, *oh*, and *so*.

One of the major differences between the two corpora is the intensity with which these features occur in *Friends*. When searching for two or three features at the same time with the concordancer, a large number of matches are easily found in *Friends*; in conversation, the co-occurrence tends to be in one of the turns and much less frequent.[6] Another salient difference is the way utterances tend to be incomplete or interrupted in conversation, as in (13). Interestingly, despite the incompleteness of these utterances, hardly ever do interlocutors indicate lack of comprehension. This phenomenon occurs because, in conversation, most exchanges involve a limited number of interlocutors who tend to share all the necessary background knowledge to ascertain comprehension. This same natural incompleteness would not be desirable in *Friends*, as, in a certain sense, the real interlocutors of the characters are the audience – millions of people with different levels of background knowledge not only of the show and the characters, but also of the world in general (see Chapter 5, Section 5.2.1 for a summary of Evison et al.'s (2007) discussion of levels of shared context).

---

6. MonoConc 2.2 has 'wild cards' that allow the user to search for particular terms separated by a pre-established number of words from each other (0–9).

6.2.3   Copular verbs *look*, *feel*, and *sound*

In addition to the more obvious features discussed above, several other linguistic features are instrumental in the expression of emotions, emphasis, and stance. It is the interaction of these features that characterizes an exchange as emotional or emphatic. In Figure 6.2, several of these features are grouped, except for the non-minimal responses (McCarthy, 2002) *sure* and *fine*, and expletives, which are described in the following sections. All of these features are significantly more frequent in *Friends*, except for *all*. As I explained in Chapter 3, Section 3.6, even though *all* was not significantly more frequent in *Friends* from a statistical point of view, it is included here because it seems to contribute to the overall more emotional nature of *Friends* as compared to conversation.

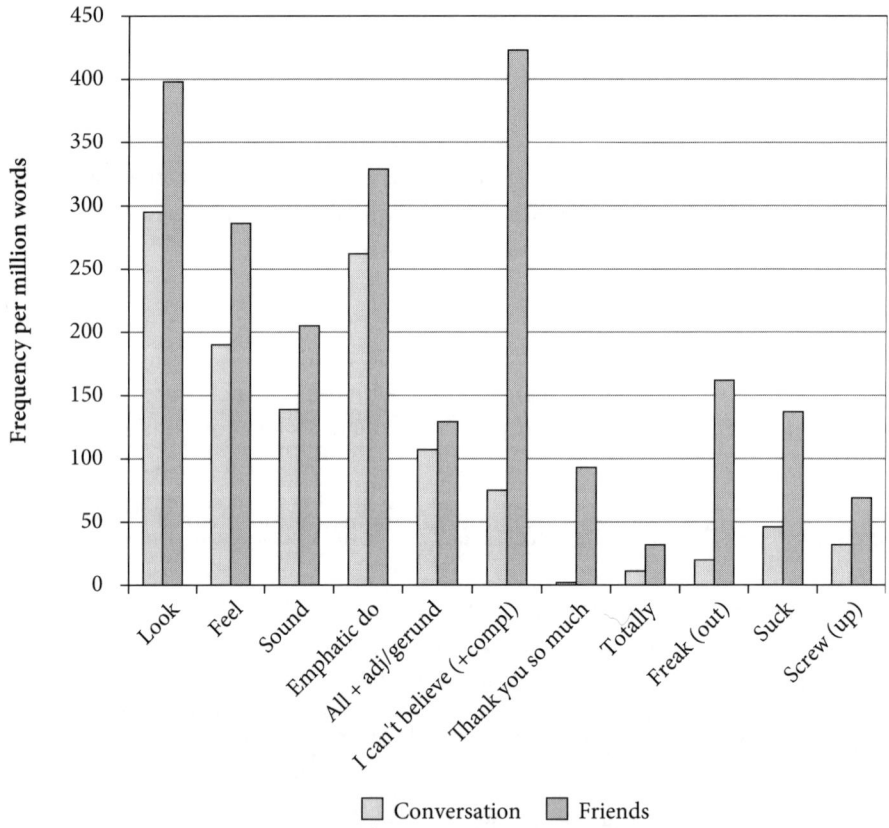

Figure 6.2 Additional features associated with emotional language

The association of the copular verbs *look, feel*, and *sound* with emotional/emphatic content might not be immediately obvious if these verbs are analyzed in isolation. However, as the authors in LGSWE point out "the sensory copular verbs... report positive or negative evaluation associated with sense perceptions. The copular verb itself identifies the sense (e.g., sight, hearing, etc), while the adjective occurring as subject predicative reports the evaluation" (p. 442). *Look* occurs 398 times/million words in *Friends* and 295 times/million words in conversation. In *Friends, look* is often associated with personal compliments. In (14), *look* is followed by the evaluative adjective *beautiful* and intensified by the adverbial *really*. Compliments are obviously frequent in conversation, but evaluations tend to be less direct and more often related to impersonal situations or inanimate objects, as in (15). This difference is clearly related to situational factors that characterize both registers. In *Friends*, most interactions involve close friends, and most topics revolve around dating, love, and close relationships, thus being much more likely to involve private issues and personal concerns.

(14) Mike: You <u>look</u> really beautiful.
      Phoebe: Thanks, you <u>look</u> good too. (*Friends*)

(15) A: We still gotta paint a lot of it. Like all this and the trim. <unclear> the doors. These doors are horrendous.
      B: As far as the paint [on]
      A: [They] just <u>look</u> so bad. (Conversation)

Feel (286 times/million words in *Friends*; 190 times/million words in conversation) also reflects evaluation, especially at the personal level. It involves emotion more closely related to personal feelings than emphatic intent. In (16), *feel* collocates with *great* in an exclamatory statement. The response to this statement includes the discourse marker *wow* and the intensifier *really*. Once again this 'linguistic collaboration' reveals the emotional/emphatic atmosphere at the discourse level in which different interlocutors co-construct the nature of the exchange.

(16) Phoebe: Hey, look who's up! How do you <u>feel</u>?
      Ross: I <u>feel</u> great. I <u>feel</u>- great, I <u>feel</u> great!
      Monica: Wow, those pills really worked, huh? (*Friends*)

The copular *sound* (205 times/million words in *Friends*; 139 times/million words in conversation) is usually used as a reaction to a suggestion or an invitation or as an integral part of an evaluative comment in *Friends*. In (17), *sound* is used as a response to a suggestion and is followed by the predicative adjective *great*. Obviously, the semantic nature of the adjective following the copular *sound* contributes to the emotional tone of the statement. In *Friends*, the most frequent right collocates of *sound* are: *great, really, so, good,* and *crazy*. In (18), *sound* is used to convey the speaker's evaluation of her own utterance and is 'surrounded' by *really* and *feel*.

(17) Phoebe: ... Listen why don't we just um, sit and relax? You know just be with each other. Quietly!

   Parker: That <u>sounds</u> great. (*Friends*)

(18) Rachel: Ok, I know this is gonna <u>sound</u> really stupid, but I feel that if I can do this, you know, if I can actually do my own laundry, there isn't anything I can't do. (*Friends*)

6.2.4 Emphatic *do*

Auxiliary *do* in emphatic position (329 times/million words in *Friends*; 262 times/ million words in conversation), as in (19), has the obvious function of emphasizing a proposition. It is found in all registers described in LGSWE (i.e., conversation, fiction, news, academic prose), but is most common in conversation and fiction (p. 433). This syntactic feature is associated with one of the discourse circumstances of conversation, the expression of stance (LGSWE, p. 1047). In (20), it co-occurs with the copular *feel* intensifying its effect since *feel*, due to its semantic nature, is closely associated with the expressions of feelings, thus suggesting emotional involvement.

(19) Monica: Yeah, I <u>do</u> think it's better this way. (*Friends*)

(20) Ross: See there, you uh, alright, ya, you did what I said.

   Rachel: Yeah, and you know what? You're right, I <u>do</u> feel better, thank you Ross. (*Friends*)

6.2.5 *All* (+ adjective/gerund) and *totally* (emphatic agreement)

All followed by an adjective or less frequently by a gerund and *totally* as an emphatic expression of agreement are also discussed in Chapter 7 as markers of informality. Here, they are analyzed for their inherently emphatic characteristics. This relatively new use of *all* in American English (129 times/million words in *Friends*; 107 times/million words in conversation) is described by Waksler (2001) as "a marker of the speaker's upcoming unique characterization of some entity in the discourse" (p. 128). This characterization is typically emphatic in nature and has an adverbial function both locally and at the overall discourse level. In (21), *all* intensifies the adjective it precedes (*happy*); in (22), its emphatic content seems to spread to the whole chunk of discourse following it.

(21) Rachel: …Ugh, you know what makes it so much worse, Ross is <u>all</u> happy in Vermont! (*Friends*)

(22) Chandler: What are you talking about?
      Joey: She was <u>all</u> crying. She-she said you guys want different things, and that and that she needed time to think. (*Friends*)

Another fairly recent innovation in American English conversation is the use of the adverb *totally* not as an adverbial intensifier but as a self-contained expression of emphatic agreement similar to *absolutely*, as in (23). It never occurs in the first turn of an interaction; rather, it is a response and typically occurs by itself. Semantically, it expresses more than simply "*I agree with you;*" it also shows stance in that it suggests agreement without any restrictions. In addition to an expression of agreement, *totally* can express an affirmative answer (meaning *I sure do/did*), as in (24), a positive response (meaning *Not a problem at all*), as in (25), or can simply be used as a non-minimal response, as in (26), with the function of backchannel. *Totally* is 3 times more frequent in *Friends*, occurring 32 times/million words; in conversation, it occurs only11 times/million words.

(23) Chandler: That's a great idea! We can easily think of a way for us both to enjoy the room.
      Monica: <u>Totally!</u> (*Friends*)

(24) Rachel: What? What!?! You kissed him?
      Phoebe: <u>Totally</u>. (*Friends*)

(25) Ross: Eh, no problem.
      Rachel: I'm gonna need a copy of those.
      Ross: <u>Totally</u>. (*Friends*)

(26) A: Like you know what fucks with my head the most? Is that Shaque is like twenty-one or twenty-two and he's actually like way younger than me. But like if I was in the room, no, you're a man and I'm kind of a little boy. <nv_laugh>
      B: <nv_laugh> <u>Totally</u>.
      A: No, do you know what I mean? Like, like it trips me out that I can be like older people that are taller than me. (Conversation)

6.2.6 Lexical bundles *I can't believe* (+ complements) and *thank you so much*

Conversation relies heavily on prefabricated sequences of words (e.g., *I don't know how*; *I don't think so*) referred to as *lexical bundles* in LGSWE and defined as "a recurrent sequence of three or more words" (p. 990).[7] The authors operationalized "recurrent" as sequences that occurred at least 10 times per million words in a particular register; in addition, these multi-word sequences had to be found in at least five different texts in the register.[8] Speakers have to produce language in real time with virtually no time to plan or edit their utterances. These "lexical building blocks" (LGSWE, p. 185) facilitate real-time production and have important discourse functions as well (Biber, Conrad, & Cortes, 2004).

I can't believe followed by its complements (e.g., *you, it, that*) and *thank you so much* are two of the most frequent lexical bundles in *Friends*. The former is over 5 times more frequent in *Friends* (423 times/million words); it occurs only 75 times/ million words in conversation. *Thank you so much* occurs 45 times/million in *Friends* and only 2 times/million in conversation. Interestingly, both bundles are associated with the pronouns *I* and *you*, suggesting personal involvement; both are used emphatically. In (27) *I can't believe you* is part of an expression of indignation. *Thank you so much* (28) contains the pronouns *I* (elided), *you*, and the adverbial intensifier *so*. As such, it is a strong reflection of involved, emphatic content. Similar to the personal involvement element I brought up in the discussion of copular verbs, *I can't believe* collocates with *you*, as in (29), only 13 times/million words in conversation; this collocation is over 8 times more frequent in *Friends*, occurring 109 times/million words.

(27)   Monica: I can't believe you didn't tell me.
        Phoebe: Oh, c'mon, like you tell me everything. (*Friends*)

(28)   Ross: Thank you so much for coming back over.
        Monica   Oh good, you're here…. (*Friends*).

(29)   A: So that's what a girl likes?
        B: No.
        A: A girl likes a guy forcing himself on her.
        B: I can't believe you said that.
        A: Well, it's only the truth. (Conversation)

---

7.   Lexical bundles are extensively discussed in LGSWE in Chapter 13 (pp. 990–1024). It should be noted that different terminology has been used to refer to these "clusters" (Scott, 1997), "recurrent word-combinations" (Altenberg, 1998), or "n-grams" (Banerjee & Pedersen, 2003), for example.

8.   Other studies have used more conservative cut-off frequency rates. Cortes (2004), for example, set her minimal cut-off rate at 20 times per million words; Biber, Conrad, and Cortes (2004) analyzed sequences occurring at least 40 times per million words.

6.2.7 Expletives and slang terms

Expletives and/or taboo terms are also associated with informality, but some of them seem to be more strongly associated with emotionally-loaded language. Like Stenström (1991), in this analysis I lump together expressions or words commonly referred to as expletives, taboo words, and swearwords and refer to them as *expletives*. Expletives in general are strongly associated with the expression of emotion; they "are realized by taboo words related to religion, sex and the human body, which are used figuratively and express the speaker's (genuine or pretended) emotions and attitudes" (Stenström, 1991, p. 240). Figure 6.3 displays the frequency of the expletives used *both* in conversation and *Friends* (*shit* and *fuck* are not used in *Friends*). Surprisingly, all of these expletives are significantly more frequent in *Friends*. Overall, *damn* (+ variations) occurs almost twice more frequently in *Friends*, 190 times/million words; in conversation, it occurs 97 times/million words. The use of these expletives is illustrated below with examples from *Friends*.

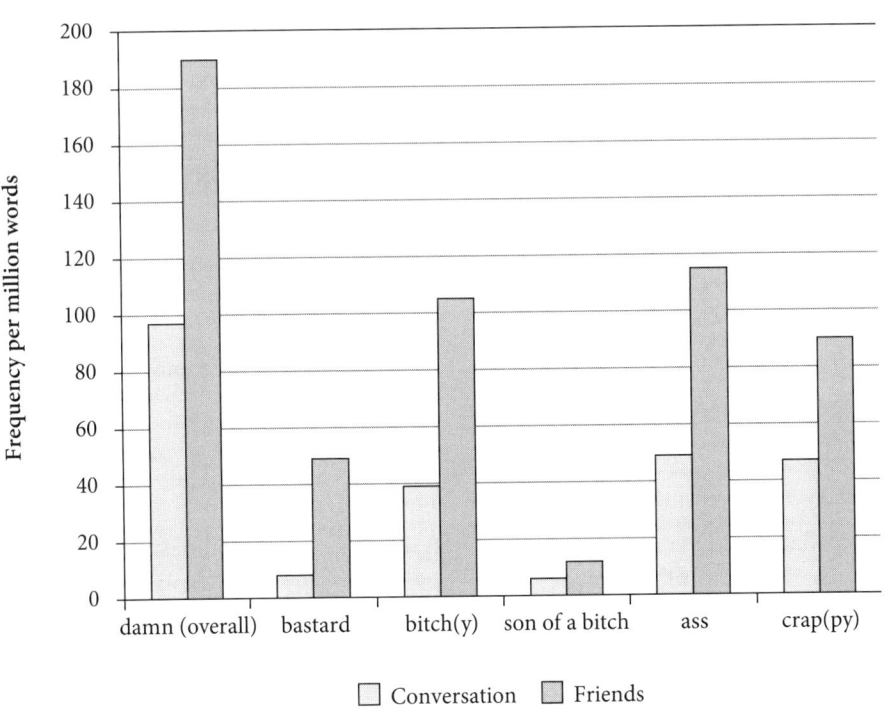

Figure 6.3 Frequency of expletives associated with emotional/emphatic content

(30) Monica: <u>Damnit</u> Ross, get your <u>butt</u> out of the bathroom.
        Ross: Calm down, I'm blow-drying. (*Friends*)

(31) Mrs.Geller: Well what is it? Come on sweetie, you're like, freaking me out here.
        Ross: I hate Chandler, the <u>bastard</u> ruined my life. (*Friends*)

(32) Ross: Well ah, Aunt Silvia was, well not a nice person.
        Monica: Oh, she was a cruel, cranky, old <u>bitch</u>! (*Friends*)

(33) Chandler: All right! Go left! Go left! Go right!! Go right!!
        Phoebe: I can't!! I can't!! Noooooooo!!!!!!! You <u>son of a bitch</u>!!!!! (*Friends*)

In (30), Monica expresses her emotional attitude through the use of *damnit*, which is acknowledged by the interlocutor (*Calm down…*). *Bastard* is 6 times more frequent in *Friends* (49 times/million words versus 8 times/million words in conversation); *bitch* (and variations) is 2.7 times more frequent in *Friends* (105 times/million words versus 39 times/million words in conversation); and *son of a bitch* is twice more frequent in *Friends* (12 times/million words versus 6 times/million words in conversation). The use of *bastard*, as in (31), *bitch* as in (32), and *son of a bitch*, as in (33) also reflect the speakers' emotions and feelings.

Because this chapter is focused on emotional/emphatic content, the occurrences of *ass* are limited to those used figuratively as part of an expression (e.g., *kick your ass*; *get your ass back here*) and not as a reference to the part of the body (e.g., *Ok, you're gonna have to not touch my ass*). Overall, *ass* is used 191 times/million words in *Friends*. Out of this total, it occurs 115 times/million words figuratively, as in (34). Interestingly, out of the124 times/million words that *butt* (a mild expletive) is used, only 19 times is it used as part of an expression as also illustrated in example (30). This seems to accentuate the preference for 'stronger language' in the expression of emotional content.

(34) Joey: Alright, you're on. I can take two minutes out of my day to kick your <u>ass</u>. (*Friends*)

Crap, illustrated in (35), is twice more frequent in *Friends* (90 times/million words versus 47 times/million words in conversation) and seems to explain an interesting phenomenon. Since *shit* is not used at all in *Friends* due to restrictions imposed by the television network, *crap* is overused in an apparent attempt to compensate for the impossibility of using the much more frequent *shit*. *Shit* is the second most frequent expletive in conversation (losing only to *fuck* + variations), occurring 244 times/million words.

(35)   Chandler: Ho, ho, ho, holy <u>crap</u> is it hot in here!
       Joey: Really, hey, you mind if I turn the heat down? (*Friends*)

It should be noted that the difference between slang terms and expletives is not clear-cut, depending on socio-cultural perceptions that speakers have of language use (see Wachal, 2002 for a discussion of what is "Taboo or not taboo"). Due to their semantic nature, *suck*, *screw* (*up*), and *pissed* (*off*) tend to reflect emotional behaviors and, because of their pervasive use, seem to have the status of slang in American English more often than that of expletive. In (35), *suck* (137 times/million words in *Friends*; 46 times/million words in conversation) is preceded by *I can't believe it*, a frequent four-word lexical bundle (54 occurrences/million words) also associated with emotional content in *Friends*. In (36), in an argument between Frank and Phoebe, *screwed up* (69 times/million words in *Friends*; 32 times/million words in conversation) is followed by the intensifier *so* modifying *bad*. Out of these three slang terms, only *pissed* (*off*) was more frequent in conversation, occurring 44 times/million words; in *Friends pissed* (*off*) occurs 13 times/million words, as in (37). Because of its semantic nature, *freak* (*out*) (= panic) is obviously a marker of emotional content. Exemplified in (38) and (39), it is eight times more frequent in *Friends*, occurring 155 times/million words; in *Friends*, it often occurs in exclamatory utterances and co-occurs with other markers of emotional language, such as adverbial intensifiers *totally* and *really*.

(35)   Joey: I can't believe it, Ross. This <u>sucks</u>! (*Friends*)

(36)   Frank: Oh, wait, no you're right, no it was perfect and I can't believe that I <u>screwed</u> it <u>up</u> so bad.
       Phoebe: You really thought it was perfect? (*Friends*)

(37)   Joey: Hey. (smiles, Ross just ignores him and turns back round) Ross, I know you're <u>pissed</u> at me, but we have to talk about this, ah actually we don't, (Ross walks off) fine, fine OK but I gotta say technically, I didn't even do anything wrong.
       Ross: (turns back) What! (angry) You didn't do anything wrong?! (*Friends*)

(38)   Rachel: Okay. Alright. Honey listen. When I tell you what I'm about to tell you, I need you to remember that we are all here for you and that we love you.
       Monica: Okay, you're-you're really <u>freaking me out</u>. (*Friends*)

(39)   A: That's weird.
       B: Spooky.
       A: Mhm. I almost like <u>freaked myself out</u> last night so I can't deal with anything scary. (Conversation)

6.2.8 Non-minimal responses *sure*, *wow*, and *fine*

Tottie (1991b) defines backchannels as "the sounds (and gestures) made in conversation by the current non-speaker, which grease the wheels of conversation but constitute no claim to take over the turn" (p. 255). The term *backchannel*, coined by Yngve (1970), has been used in reference to vocalizations, such as *Mm* and *Uh-huh*, single-word responses, such as *Yeah*, *Right*, *Oh*, *Sure*, and multiple-word responses, such as *That's right*, *I see*, and *Oh dear*. Carter and McCarthy (2006) use the umbrella term "response token" and offer the following definition:

> Word or phrase used to acknowledge what a speaker says, and to indicate on the part of the listener interest or engagement in what is being said. Response tokens include minimal response tokens (sounds or words like oh, mm, yeah, okay, no), and non-minimal response tokens, which are frequently made up of adjectives and adverbs or short phrases or clauses (great, exactly, very good, that's true). (p. 922)

In this analysis, the single-word responses *Sure*, *Wow*, and *Fine* were included. I refer to these backchannel instances as non-minimal responses (McCarthy, 2002). Non-minimal responses have an important function in conversation: they indicate interest in or comprehension of the interlocutor's utterance and thus signal good listenership (ibid.). *Sure*, *wow*, and *fine* are some of the response tokens showing a significant difference in distribution in the comparison between American and British English carried out by McCarthy (ibid.). *Sure* and *wow* were found to be more frequent in American English. *Sure*, a stance marker indicating certainty, is here analyzed as a *non-minimal response*, as in (40). With this function, *sure* occurs 80 times/million words in *Friends* and 66 times/million words in conversation. For this analysis, *wow*, as in (41), was classified as a non-minimal response when it occurred by itself in the turn, being directly followed by the interlocutor's turn (all instances were included in Section 6.2.2). Out of the three non-minimal responses chosen for analysis of emotional content, only *wow* was more frequent in conversation, occurring 130 times/million words, whereas *Friends* yielded 90 instances/million words. *Fine* (found to be more frequent in British English in McCarthy's study) with the function of non-minimal response is 10 times more frequent in *Friends*, occurring 32 times/million words versus only 3 times/million words in conversation. Interestingly, almost all of the instances of *fine* in *Friends* were part of confrontational situations in which the characters were involved. *Fine* here does not have a positive meaning; it is used as a sign of defiance as in (42) and is, obviously, emotionally loaded.

(40)   Joey: Come on! You like this woman, right?
        Ross: Yeah.

	Joey:	You want to see her again, right?
	Ross:	Sure. (*Friends*)
(41)	A:	That is a nice Mustang, have you seen it?
	B:	Right there, the red one
	A:	Wow
	B:	Yeah, it's pretty cool... (Conversation)
(42)	Rachel:	What? Come on, you do what you want to do. Do we always have to do everything together?
	Monica:	You know what? You're right.
	Phoebe:	Fine!
	Ross:	Fine! (*Friends*)

6.3 Summary

The emotional/emphatic content of utterances can be easily perceived through the interlocutors' tone of voice or typical intonation patterns. Unless the corpus is annotated for prosodic features, these indicators cannot be quantified. This chapter has focused on the linguistic markers of emotionally-loaded language. The frequency-based analysis of these markers reveals that the language of *Friends* tends to be more emotional and emphatic than conversation. This 'dramatic' effect is linguistically realized by high frequencies of several features associated with (but not limited to) emotionally-loaded language. These features are found not only interspersed in the dialogues but also in the same or immediately preceding or following turn. The co-occurrence of these features in the same turn suggests that they share the same or very similar functions; when the emotionally-loaded atmosphere is created by different speakers, this co-occurrence reflects the collaborative nature of conversation in which the interaction is co-constructed by the participants of the communicative event.

I have shown that emotionally-loaded features are easily found close to each other, as part of the preceding or subsequent turn in *Friends*. The overuse of expletives in *Friends* is surprising, considering that the show is aired in prime time. The absence, in *Friends*, of the two most frequent expletives in conversation, *shit* and *fuck*, is one of the differences resulting from restrictions imposed by the television network. Finally, several features are more frequent in *Friends* due to situational factors, as the characters share close relationships and topics tend to revolve around dating, love, and romantic relationships. One of these features is the copular *look*, which tends to involve personal evaluative comments; in conversation, *look* tends to be more impersonal and often relates to inanimate entities.

CHAPTER 7

I'm just hanging out. Y'know, having fun

Informal language

Ross:	<u>Dude</u>, we are *so* <u>gonna</u> party!
Phoebe:	Wow! Okay, dude alert! And who is this guy?
Ross:	Mike "Gandolf" Ganderson, only like the funest guy in the world.
Chandler:	I'm <u>gonna</u> call and get off work tomorrow!
Ross:	I'm <u>gonna</u> call after you!
Chandler:	This is <u>gonna</u> be so <u>cool</u>, <u>dude</u>, we never party anymore!

[*Friends*: Season 4, episode 9 – The One Where They're Gonna Party]

A:	<u>Dude</u>, Brian's so <u>cool</u>, I'm really shy and stuff and I hate pornography and <u>shit</u> like that but, I felt so trusting with him, we made a movie one night.
B:	Really?
A:	With his studio camera. It's like, make sure that tape doesn't go to the <u>fucking</u> studio, okay? It was funny though. (Conversation)

7.1 Introduction

What makes language informal or colloquial? What does it mean when a teacher tells her student, "Your essay *sounds* too informal?" In Chapter 4, I presented the results of the multidimensional (MD) analysis (Biber, 1988) of *Friends* and discussed the striking similarities between *Friends* and natural conversation. I showed that involved (interactive) registers, such as natural conversation, are characterized by the presence of specific sets of co-occurring linguistic features. The presence of features, such as private verbs (e.g., *think, believe*), *that*-deletion (*I think ø she's coming tomorrow*), contractions, present tense verbs, first- and second-person pronouns, *be* as main verb, and causative subordination is, in fact, part of what makes language *sound* informal. The short excerpt below has several of these features: four first-person pronouns, one *that*-deletion (*I think this is...*), two private verbs (*think, know*), two instances of *be* as main verb (*is, are*), present tense verbs (*is, are, have, know*), and an example of causative subordination (*because none of…*). These are some of the *core* linguistic features that characterize involved registers or *informal language.*

Monica:	I think this is so cool because none of our friends are here and we can be a real couple. We don't have to hide.
Chandler:	I know, I can do this. (He takes her hand.)
Monica:	Ooh, and I can do this. (She kisses him on the cheek.) (*Friends*)

In addition to these linguistic features, several other features have been analyzed as markers of informality. The two excerpts from *Friends* and conversation at the beginning of this chapter present some of these markers: vocatives (familiarizers) (*dude*), semi-modals (*gonna*), an instance of 'language innovation' (*so* modifying a verb), and the slang term *cool*. In addition, two examples of expletives are found in the conversation excerpt: *shit* and *fucking*. The co-occurrence of these features reflects informality; the frequency of these features can thus be interpreted as a measure of the *degree* of informality of a particular text. In this chapter, I take a closer look at these additional markers of informality, describe them, and compare them in *Friends* and conversation.

7.2 The linguistic expression of informality

The analysis of the linguistic features associated with informality reveals one of the most consistent differences between *Friends* and conversation. Table 7.1 shows that of the 35 features chosen for analysis, 31 were more frequent in *Friends*, one presented similar counts, and only three were more common in conversation.

Before I provide the frequency counts as well as examples of these features, a note is in order. As I explained in Chapter 3, linguistic features can be associated with different discourse functions. Most expletives and some slang terms can be associated with *both* emotional language and informality. For example, the mild expletive *crap*, as in (1), conveys this sense of informality but also reflects emotional content. To provide the reader with a more thorough picture of the analysis, I include the same table of expletives here with the addition of *shit* and *fuck*. By the same token, the borderline expletives/slang terms *suck*, *pissed* (*off*), and *screwed*(*up*), analyzed in Chapter 6 along with other features reflecting emotional language, are also included here along with several other slang terms, such as *cool* and *What's up?*, as markers of informality.

(1)   A: Oh really, oh no I don't want that, I want it with tomatoes. 'Cause I love tomatoes

B: Um Nadia wants, Nadia, oh crap I've just spilled it… (Conversation)

Table 7.1 Features associated with informal language

Category	Feature	Conversation	*Friends*	Similar
Expletives	Damn; Bastard; Bitch(y)		•	
	Son of a bitch		•	
	Shit(ty); Fuck (+ var.)	•		
	Ass; Butt; Crap(py)		•	
Slang terms	Piss(ed)(off)	•		
	Screw(ed)(up)		•	
	Suck; Check out; Hang out		•	
	Cool; Totally		•	
	What's up?; Freak out		•	
Vocatives	Guys; Man; Dude; Buddy		•	
	Folks; Bro; Bud			•
Innovations	All + adj/gerund		•	
	So + verb		•	
	So (not) + NP		•	
	So not + Adj		•	
	IN +neg pres perf+ time		•	
Semi-modals	e.g., (have) got to, (had) better		•	
Repeats	e.g., I-I-I		•	
Greetings & leave-takings	Hi; Hey; Bye + bye-bye		•	

7.2.1 Expletives

As explained in the analysis of markers of emotionally-loaded language (Chapter 6, Section 6.2.7), like Stenström (1991), I use the cover term *expletive* to refer to taboo or swearwords in general. Carter and McCarthy (2006) explain that "the use of taboo words and phrases projects either a close, intimate relationship with the person or group to whom they are addressed (so that one feels free to use taboo words) or else a threatening and hostile relationship" (p. 225). Along with slang terms, expletives are probably the most obvious markers of informality (Cooper, 2001). As shown in Figure 7.1, except for *shit* and *fuck*, all of the expletives chosen for analysis were more frequent in *Friends*.

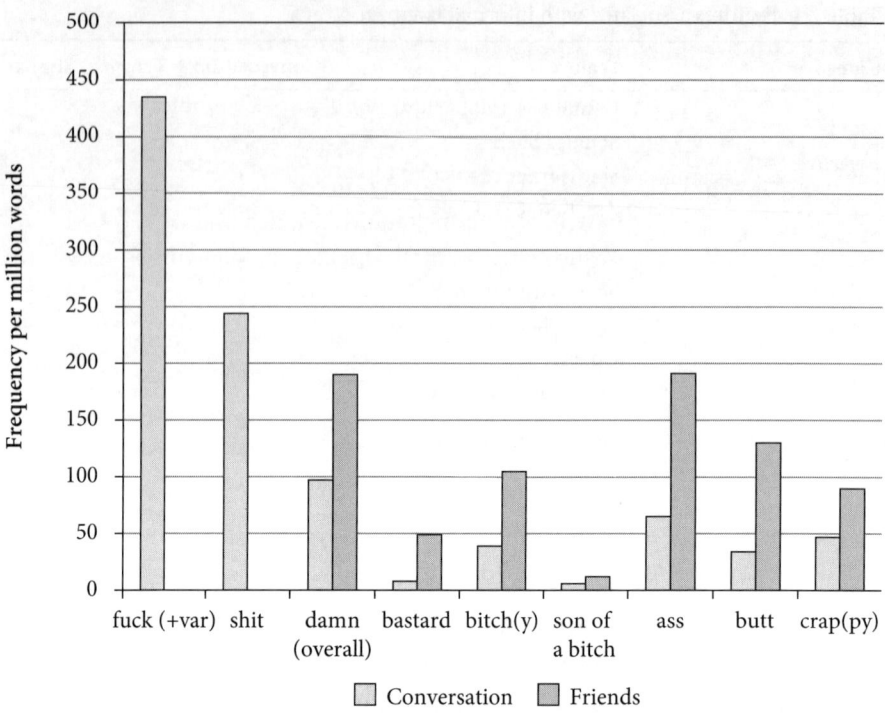

Figure 7.1 Frequency of expletives in *Friends* vs. conversation

The use of most of the expletives shown in Figure 7.1 was discussed and exemplified in Chapter 6. In this chapter, I provide examples of and comment on those expletives that were not addressed in Chapter 6. *Shit* and *fuck*, by far the most frequent expletives in conversation, are not present is *Friends*. This absence is clearly due to restrictions imposed by the televised medium and/or the television network. *Fuck* (+ variations) occurs 435 times/million words in conversation; *shit* occurs 244 times/million words. It is important to emphasize that the use of expletives does not necessarily result in the production of insults; they are often used for the "establishment of an informal, friendly atmosphere between interlocutors" (Quaglio & Biber, 2006, p. 712). In the conversation corpus, they often occur with the transcriber's note <*laugh*>, denoting informality, as in (2). In example (3), *fucking* is used as an adverbial intensifier twice; the second time, it modifies *shit*, which is used as a noun of vague reference in this context. In (4), the two instances of *shit* are used as interjections. As shown in Chapter 6, the borderline expletive/slang term *pissed off* is the only term in this category that is more frequent in conversation (when considering terms that occur in both corpora), occurring 44 times/million words and only 13 times/million words in *Friends*). Notice how it co-occurs with and is intensified by *fucking* in example (5) from conversation. Example (6) illustrates the use of *pissed* in *Friends*.

(2) A: He's gonna create it too and we'll all finally be fabulously wealthy.
     B: <u>Fuck you</u>. <laugh>
     A: <laugh> (Conversation)

(3) A: Did they have it, they didn't require any cleaning.
     B: That is so <u>fucking</u> weird. All this <u>fucking</u> <u>shit</u> hanging from the ceiling. Alright, let's uh, let's stick it here. (Conversation).

(4) A: That means we're not going to a haunted house tomorrow night?
     B: <u>Shit</u>! Tomorrow's Halloween. <u>Shit</u>! No we have to go. (Conversation)

(5) A: ...they ran out of beer at about eleven o'clock.
     B: I know I was <u>fucking pissed off</u>. (Conversation)

(6) Joey: Uh, I think she's still asleep. Hey, hey, how did it go with you guys last night? She seemed pretty <u>pissed</u> at you.
     Ross: Uh, we, y'know, we worked things out. (*Friends*)

One of the most interesting differences between *Friends* and conversation in the use of expletives is that, in *Friends*, even though they do add to the perception of informality, they tend to be used to convey emotional content, whereas, in conversation, they are more often associated with the expression of informality. This difference seems to stem from two factors: the conversation corpus, probably due to data collection limitations, may not have captured the more intensely emotional exchanges that seem to be typical of *Friends*. In addition, the restricted set of relationship types (mostly intimate and extremely casual) as well as limited settings and interaction types in *Friends* seem to be responsible for the lack of balance in the effect naturally brought about by the use of expletives.

7.2.2   Slang terms

In Chapter 6, the mild expletive *ass* and the milder *butt* were analyzed as part of expressions, such as *kick your ass* and *bring you butt back here*, and mainly occur in emotionally-loaded contexts. With its original lexical meaning (a part of the body), *ass* and *butt* are usually markers of informality. For example, when speakers choose to use *ass* instead of *buttocks*, they indicate that they hope to keep the tone of the conversation informal and casual. In *Friends*, exemplified in (7), the use of *ass* reflects the informality of the exchange and the casual atmosphere commonly shared by close friends.

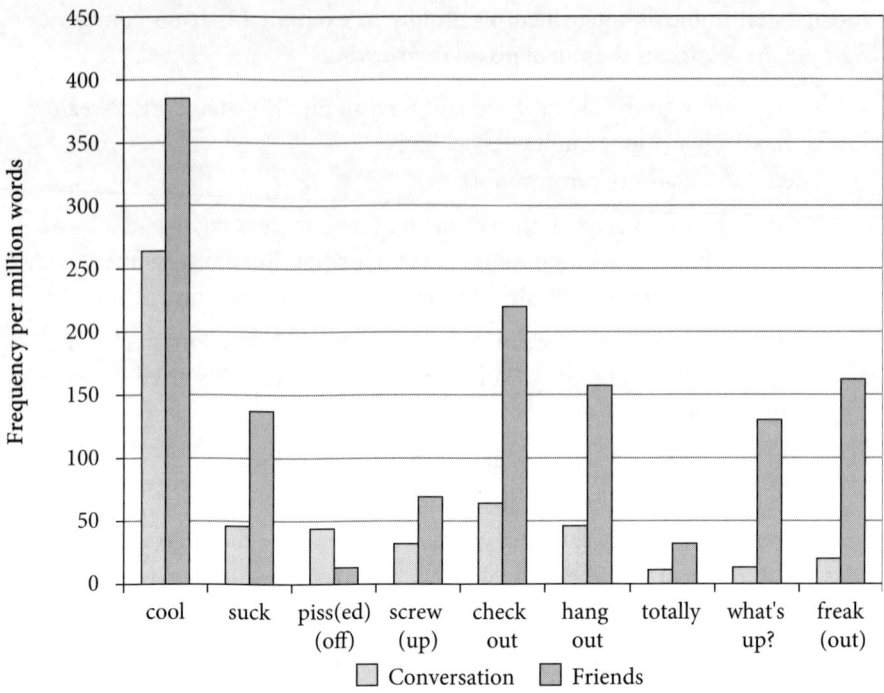

Figure 7.2 Frequency of slang terms in *Friends* vs. conversation

(7)   Rachel: Oh, come on squeeze it.
Ross: No.
Rachel: Rub it.
Ross: No.
Rachel: Oh, come on, would you just grab my <u>ass</u>.

Figure 7.2 shows that, except for *pissed* (*off*), all of the slang terms chosen for analysis are more frequent in *Friends*. *Cool* is the most frequent slang term in *Friends*, occurring 385 times/million words; in conversation, it occurs 264 times/million words. *Suck* is 3 times more frequent in *Friends* and, like *cool*, is often associated with emotionally-loaded language. In (8), *cool* is modified by the intensifier *so*; in (9), *suck* co-occurs with *cool*, which is modified by *really*. The combination of slang (as a marker of informality) and adverbial intensifiers seems to accentuate the informality of the exchange. Interestingly, the most frequent left collocates of *cool* in *Friends* are the intensifiers *so*, *really*, and *pretty*. When considered together, *cool* is modified by adverbial intensifiers at a rate of 47 times/million words; even though in conversation the top left collocates of *cool* are also adverbial intensifiers (*really* and *pretty*), they modify *cool* at a lower rate, 29 times/million words.

(8) Monica: Y'know what, I like Kathy.
    Chandler: Oh yeah, me too, she's so <u>cool</u> and pretty. (*Friends*)

(9) Monica: …You know for a really <u>cool</u> guy, you <u>suck</u> at foosball.
    Richard: What're you talkin' about, I was killin' 'em.
    Monica: Yeah, well they <u>suck</u> too. (*Friends*)

Hang out (10) and *what's up?* are examples of slang expressions that are not associated with emotional language; rather, they are associated with the situational circumstances of *Friends*. This is a show in which, most of the time, people spend time together (*hang out*) and *talk*. The expression *What's up?* is 10 times more frequent in *Friends*, occurring 130 times/million words; it is often an integral part of a greeting, as in (11), and is also used for clarification purposes, as in (12), with the slangy meaning of *What's going on? Freak* (*out*) is certainly a marker of informality but seems to be more strongly associated with emotional language and was discussed in Chapter 6.

(10) Monica: What-what are you doing?
    Chandler: I'm just <u>hanging out</u>. Y'know, having fun. (*Friends*)

(11) Rachel: (entering) Hey guys! <u>What's up</u>?
    Joey: Hey
    Monica: We're hanging out. (*Friends*)

(12) Nina: Do you have a sec?
    Chandler: Ah, sure, Nina. <u>What's up?</u> (*Friends*)

Totally, as in (13), is 3 times more frequent in *Friends*, occurring 32 times/million words. A fairly recent innovation of American English, it does not have its canonical meaning (i.e., completely) in this context, thus not functioning as an adverbial intensifier; it is used to express emphatic agreement and often occurs as a non-minimal response (McCarthy, 2002). This use of *totally* illustrates an apparent process of language change in progress (or at least the addition of a new function to the word). This linguistic innovation also adds to the informal nature of *Friends* (see discussion of *totally* as an adverbial intensifier in Chapter 6, Section 6.2.1).

(13) Rachel: I'm gonna need a copy of those.
    Ross: <u>Totally</u>. (*Friends*)

7.2.3 Vocatives (Familiarizers)

In English, address forms are not grammatically marked for degrees of formality (through the use of personal pronouns, for example); they are linguistically realized through the use of vocatives. LGSWE (pp. 1108–1113) lists several categories of vocatives ranging from terms of endearment (e.g., *honey*, *sweetie*) to the more formal honorifics (e.g., *sir*, *madam*). As Leech (1999) puts it, familiarizers (e.g., *man*, *dude*), one of these categories, "mark the relationship between speaker and addressee as a familiar one" (p. 112), thus having a "purely social bond-maintaining function" (p. 108).

(14) Monica: Hi guys!
      Joey: Hey!
      Chandler: Hey! (*Friends*)

(15) Chandler: Look, maybe we should go?
      Rachel: No, you guys, you really don't have to go… we're done talking.
                (*Friends*)

(16) Chandler: I can't believe she's married.
      Joey: Aw, man I'm sorry. This must be very tough for ya, huh.
                (*Friends*)

(17) Joey: Aww man! I can't believe I locked myself out again!
      Chandler: Hang on buddy! (*Friends*)

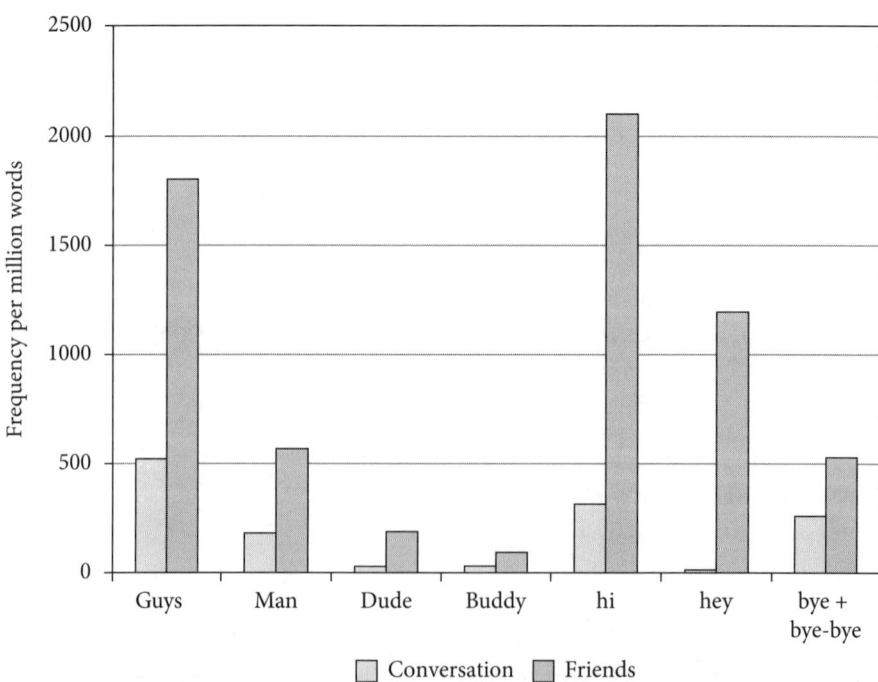

Figure 7.3 Frequency of the most common vocatives (familiarizers) and informal greetings & leave takings in *Friends* vs. conversation

(18) Chandler: This is gonna be so cool, <u>dude</u>, we never party any-
                       more!
      Chandler and Ross: Woooo!!! (*Friends*)

Figure 7.3 shows the frequency of some of the most common vocatives in conversation and *Friends*. *Guys* (almost 3.5 times more frequent in *Friends*) is used to
address more than one interlocutor and often co-occurs with greetings, as in (14).
In (15), it 'smoothes out' the pronoun *you*, suggesting closeness of relationship.
Man (16) and *buddy* (17) are both a little over 3 times more frequent in *Friends*.
Dude, the most 'slangy' of the vocatives, is much less common than *guys* and *man*
but is almost 6.5 more frequent in *Friends*. In (18), *dude* is 'surrounded' by *cool* and
the contracted semi-modal *gonna* (see Section 7.2.6), both markers of informality.

7.2.4 Informal greetings and leave-takings

Informality is also reflected in the use of informal greetings and leave-takings. The
much higher frequency of greetings in *Friends* results from a situational characteristic: several scenes begin with the characters meeting each other, which is not
captured by the conversation corpus as often. Example (14) above shows an interesting fast-paced combination of a vocative and two greetings; the disparity in the
frequency of *guys* and the greeting *hi*, for example, shows an important difference
between the two corpora; the frequent co-occurrence of these features accentuates
this situational difference.

Figure 7.3 above also shows that *hi* is over 6 times more frequent in *Friends*,
occurring 2102 times/million words. What is striking, however, is the high frequency in which the much more informal greeting *hey* is used: (1195 times/mil-
lion words in *Friends* vs. 13.5 times/million words in conversation). Considering
that the use of *hey* as a greeting is a relatively recent innovation in American English conversation, it is surprising that *hi* is just 1.7 times more frequent than *hey* in
Friends; in conversation, *hi* is 23 times more frequent than *hey*, occurring 315
times/million words. This overuse of *hey* is one of the indications of the deliberate
attempt to confer a high degree of informality to the communicative exchanges in
the show. Example (19), below, shows a brief exchange with two instances of *hey*
used as greetings, *guys* (address term denoting familiarity), followed by *what's up?*,
a slang expression. The 'collaboration' of these features contributes to and reflects
the high degree of informality that is pervasive in *Friends*.

(19) Joey: <u>Hey</u> you <u>guys</u>.
      Chandler: <u>Hey</u> Joe <u>what's up</u>? (*Friends*)

7.2.5 Linguistic innovations

In Chapter 6, I discussed the use of *all* followed by an adjective (as in *She was all happy…*) or a gerund (as in *She was all crying…*) as well as the new uses of the adverbial intensifier *totally* as markers of emotional language. Earlier in this chapter, I discussed the slangy use of *totally* as an expression of emphatic agreement – similar to *absolutely* in this context. Potentially, all of these cases of linguistic innovation also qualify as markers of informality. In this section, I focus on two syntactic innovations of American English: new functions of the adverbial modifier *so* (also a marker of emphatic content) and preposition *in* as part of a very specific syntactic environment: negative statements with present perfect aspect followed by a time expression. Figure 7.4 shows that both of these features are much more frequent in *Friends*.

Adverbial intensifier *so*, in its canonical function, modifies an adjective (as in *You're so beautiful*) or an adverb (as in *You're so incredibly beautiful*). As a linguistic innovation, *so* modifies a noun, as in (20), a verb, as in (21), and an adjective or a clause split by the negator *not*, as in (22) and (23) respectively. In these new environments, *so* is 23 times more frequent in *Friends*, occurring 70 times/million words

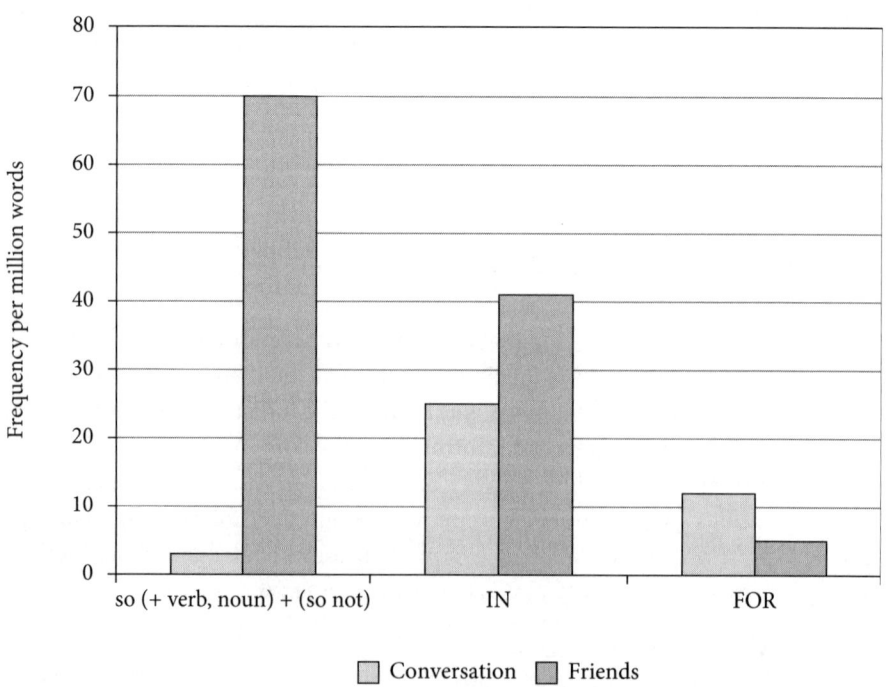

Figure 7.4 Syntactic innovation signaling informality in *Friends* vs. conversation

and only 3 times/million words in conversation. This discrepancy is probably due to the fact that the conversation corpus was collected between 1995 and 1996. This innovation then might not have been fully captured by the conversation corpus.

(20) Ross: Please. This is <u>so</u> your fault.
     Susan: How, how is this my fault? (*Friends*)

(21) A: There are days where I'<u>m</u> just like <u>so wanting</u> to capture everything I think and just feel good, it's amazing.
     B: Well that's what you've got your journal for. (Conversation)

(22) Joey: You know what the Celtics problem is? They let the players run the team.
     Lydia: Oh, that is <u>so not</u> true. (*Friends*)

(23) Ross: Hey, y'know, this is <u>so not</u> what I needed right now. (*Friends*)

This '*so* innovation' is particularly interesting in that it seems to have been popularized by *Friends*. In the internet site *Terms of the 90s, Slang of the 90s* (http://www.inthe90s.com), the following entry for *so* is found:

> So (adv. very much). Traditionally used as intensifying adverbs or adjectives, usage expanded to intensify whole clauses, predicates, phrases, etc. Usage may have gained popularity on TV's "Friends." (Chandler: "That is *so* not the opposite of taking somebody's underwear!"...Joey, jokingly: "I *so* didn't know that, but you should have seen your faces").

Similarly, one of the several online *Friends*' fan clubs makes this witty 'recommendation':

> So you wanna speak like the characters on *FRIENDS*, but can't remember all their floopy terminology? … Be sure to make liberal usage of "not" and "so": "Do we not like them?" or "You are *so* going to Minsk." Use "so" and "not" together in the same sentence and get a double whammy: "That is *so not* true!" (http://www.angelfire.com/tv/chocgal/talk.html).

Whether this is an example of the influence of the spoken media on processes of language change or simply a case of linguistic innovation that has been captured by the show scriptwriters is beyond the scope of the present study. Whatever the case, the conscious decision to make this innovation so pervasive in the show is one more indication of the deliberate attempt to portray the language of *Friends* as informal.

The preference for *in* instead of *for* in negative statements with present perfect aspect followed by a time expression, as illustrated in (24) and (25), has been described in Quaglio (2002): *in* is preferred 70 % of the time in American English conversation in this environment; the preference for *for* in the same context is almost categorical in British English conversation (98%). A follow-up public survey showed a lower preference for *in* (even though still higher than *for*) by older speakers of American English, thus suggesting that this could be a phenomenon of language change in progress. In *Friends* the preference for *in* is even higher than in conversation, reaching 89%, perhaps a reflection of the characters' ages. This construction occurs 41 times/million words in *Friends* and 25 times/million words in conversation. Notice also the reduced use of *for* in *Friends*; in conversation, the use of *for* in this environment is almost 2.6 more frequent, occurring 12 times/million words.

> (24) Monica: Relax. Y'know, she may not even know.
>   Rachel: Please. I haven't heard from her in seven months, and now she calls me? (*Friends*)
>
> (25) A: I like your skin full of sun
>   B: Oh, my eyes look really nice when my face is tan, it hasn't been that way in like seven years but... I remember when... yeah... I'll get some sun this summer ...(Conversation)

7.2.6   Semi-modals

LGSWE defines semi-modals (e.g., (*had*) *better, have to,* (*have*) *got to, be supposed to, be going to*) as "fixed idiomatic phrases with functions similar to those of modals" (p. 484). Semi-modals reflect informality at the syntactic level. In conversation, they are often used in contracted form (e.g., *gonna, gotta,* ('d) *better*), accentuating the informality of the exchanges. Semi-modals are very common in both *Friends* and conversation but are significantly more frequent in *Friends*, occurring 8445 times/million words; in conversation, they occur 7527 times/million words. Example (26) shows an exchange with two semi-modals, *gotta* and *gonna* in different turns, showing that the informality is shared by the two speakers.

> (26) Rachel: Well, we gotta find out if he's alive.
>   Monica: How are we gonna do that? There's no way. (*Friends*)

7.2.7   Repeats

Along with false starts and hesitations[1], repeats (e.g., *I-I*) are one of the features resulting from the pressures of online production. These features are typical of

---

1.   Rühlemann (2006) questions the appropriateness of labels, such as 'false start,' 'hesitation,' and 'dysfluency' to describe features of conversational grammar. He proposes the term 'speech management phenomena,' which, according to him, does not have the negative connotation that the word 'dysfluency' has. Ruhlemann argues that "speech management phenomena can be seen as adaptations to the needs arising from the interactive nature of real-time conversation" (p. 402).

conversational grammar and have important discourse functions. As Rühlemann (2006) puts it, "repeats in conversation may serve speakers and potential next speakers as effective means in the way they organize their turn-taking" (p. 402). It is important to keep in mind that the *Friends* corpus is not composed of scripts; rather, it comprises transcripts of the show, thus capturing the actors' 'linguistic realization' of the lines assigned to them. For example, actors are sometimes directed to express certain types of behaviors or attitudes that transcend the scripted dialogues (e.g., reluctantly, excitedly); they thus need to make certain linguistic choices to convey these behaviors or attitudes, and *repeats* can be instrumental for the achievements of this dramatic effect.

The presence of repeats in the *Friends* corpus seems to be related to two important factors in the construction of good dialogue: authenticity and informality. I include repeats as markers of informality because face-to-face conversation is inherently informal and interactive. Repeats tend to co-occur with highly interactive chunks of discourse. It seems plausible to conclude that the 'addition' of repeats is a deliberate attempt to make the scripted dialogues sound natural, casual, and informal. Two- (e.g., *I I*), three- (e.g., *I I I*), and four- (e.g., *I I I I*) repeats were included in the analysis. Surprisingly, these instances of "non-fluencies" (Stenström & Svartvik, 1994), "dysfluency" (LGSWE, Ch. 14), or "speech management phenomena" (Rühlemann, 2006) are almost twice more frequent in *Friends* (7937 times/million words) than in conversation (4372 times/million words), as shown in Figure 7.5 below. In (27), the instances of repeats (and also hesitators and false starts) seem to reflect Rachel's surprise (perhaps indignation) and Ross's insecurity as he tries to explain his jealous reaction. The overuse of repeats is consonant with the overall overuse of most of the features marking informality in *Friends*. It seems that in the attempt to create credible, informal dialogue, scriptwriters and actors may have wound up 'overshooting the colloquial mark.' As the analyses of vague language (Chapter 5) and emotional language (Chapter 6) have shown, humor seems to play an important role in the use and frequency of these features as well.

(27) Ross: Uh, uh, <u>you're</u>, umm, <u>you're</u> my lobster.
   Rachel: OK, you know what, <u>are</u>, <u>are</u> being like, the blind date guy again?
   Ross: <u>No no</u>, <u>you're</u> uh, <u>you're</u> my lobster. See um, lobsters, uhh, in the tank <u>when</u>, <u>when</u> they're old, uhh, they get with, uhh, they walk around holding the claws. (*Friends*)

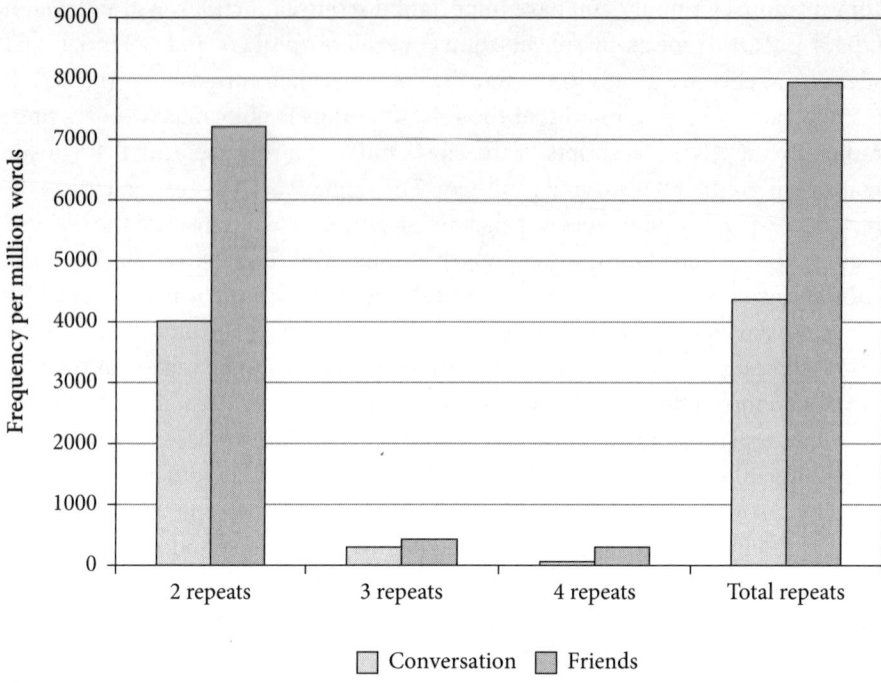

Figure 7.5 Frequency of repeats in *Friends* vs. conversation

7.3 Summary

In this chapter, I have shown that the vast majority of linguistic features associated with informal language tend to be much more frequent in *Friends*. Features such as slang terms, vocatives, greetings and leave-takings, some linguistic innovations and, surprisingly, expletives and repeats interact and reflect the high degree of informality of the dialogues in *Friends*.

The overuse of these features can be attributed to at least three factors: the attempt to make the language of *Friends* credible and authentic, the extremely close relationships shared by the characters, and the creation of humor. As discussed in the analyses of vague language and emotional language, there is some evidence that the 'idiosyncratic' use of some of the features and the overuse of others result from the 'addition' of humor, which is often created through pragmatic failure when the characters behave or react in unexpected ways. The concept of conversational sub-genres (McCarthy, 1998) should not be overlooked either. It is plausible to think that the similarities between the two corpora could be enhanced if the conversation corpus used for analysis were made up of very casual, intimate exchanges only, one of the sub-genres of conversation. Finally, the attempt by scriptwriters and actors to portray the show as highly informal or at least as informal as they perceive conversation to be in the context in which *Friends* takes place, seems to have resulted in a typical case of 'overcorrection', thus causing the dialogues in the show to become less natural than what might have been intended.

CHAPTER 8

Once upon a time

Narrative language

Phoebe: Well, but that's what <u>he</u> <u>was</u> for me. And <u>she</u> you know, kind of <u>stole</u> <u>him</u> away, and then... <u>broke</u> <u>his</u> heart... and then <u>he</u> wouldn't even talk to me any more. Because <u>he</u> <u>said</u> he <u>didn't</u> <u>wanna</u> be around... anything that <u>looked</u> like either one of us.

Rachel: Oh... Oh, Pheebs.

[*Friends*: Season 1, episode 16 – The One With Two Parts (1)]

A: <u>He</u> <u>was</u> from Poland and I'<u>d</u> <u>seen</u> when <u>he</u> <u>walked</u> in <u>he</u> was carrying this boy like, I would say the boy <u>was</u> six or seven years old maybe, and <u>he</u> was carrying <u>him</u>. <u>He</u> must be crippled or something. Well, then the, the fellow that's the head organist and choir is from Poland but <u>he</u>'s been here for ten years or so and, uh, then <u>he</u> <u>said</u> he's here with <u>his</u> son, <u>he</u>'s taking <u>him</u> to a, uh, Ann Arbor for surgery

B: Mm. (Conversation)

8.1 Introduction

Registers have a multifaceted nature; no one register has 'absolute' linguistic characteristics. For example, face-to-face conversation is linguistically characterized by a high frequency of features "marking affective, interactional, and generalized content" (Biber, Conrad, & Reppen 1998, p. 151), such as private verbs (e.g., *think*, *believe*), *that*-deletion, contractions, and present tense. These features tend to co-occur because they perform similar discourse functions. However, face-to-face conversation, like every register, has elements of narrative or persuasive discourse, for example. In other words, face-to-face conversation has a *degree* of involvement (which tends to be high), a *degree* of narrativeness (which tends to be low when compared to fiction, for example), and a *degree* of persuasiveness (which tends to be low when compared to professional letters). Therefore, as Biber, Conrad, & Reppen (1998) concluded their discussion of register variation, "register variation must be considered in a multidimensional space – ... register comparisons with respect to individual linguistic features, or along a single dimension of variation, are inadequate for a comprehensive understanding of the relationship among registers" (p. 156).

In Chapter 4, I showed the similarities between *Friends* and conversation as revealed by the results of the multidimensional analysis (Biber, 1988). Specifically, I focused on Biber's Dimension 1 (D1) (*involved versus informational production*) and the linguistic features characterizing involved registers, such as face-to-face conversation. In this chapter, I look at conversation and *Friends* from a different perspective: I focus on their narrative dimension. I discuss the linguistic expression of narrative discourse, present the results of the multidimensional analysis relative to Biber's Dimension 2 (D2) (*narrative versus non-narrative discourse*), and compare the *degrees* of narrativeness typifying each of the registers.

8.2 Narrative discourse

Biber (1988) identified several grammatical features characterizing narrative discourse: past tense verbs, third person pronouns, perfect aspect verbs, public verbs[1] (e.g., say, explain, agree, complain), synthetic negation (e.g., *she had no options available*), and present participial clauses. Similar to the two excerpts that open this chapter, the excerpt below, taken from the *Longman Grammar* fiction subcorpus, illustrates most of these features: it has several examples of past tense verbs (bold), 14 third-person pronouns (italics), seven instances of public verbs (double underlining), and three cases of perfect aspect (underlined). The high frequency of these co-occurring features confers a high degree of narrativeness to this excerpt.

> *She* **said,** `Mr Evans, I've something to tell you, something important,' and then
> **rushed** straight into it before *he* could stop *her* and say, `Clear out while I'm

Table 8.1 Descriptive statistics for *Friends* and face-to-face conversation on Biber's D1 (involved vs. informational production) and D2 (narrative vs. non-narrative discourse)

Dimension	Register	Mean	Min Value	Max Value	Range	St Dev
D1	*Friends*	34.4	23.7	45.8	22	4.3
	F-T-F Conv	35.3	17.7	54.1	36.4	9.1
D2	*Friends*	- 2.1	- 3.5	- 0.3	3.2	0.6
	F-T-F Conv	- 0.6	- 4.4	4.0	8.4	2.0

---

1.   Biber (1988) defines public verbs as those "involv[ing] actions that can be observed publicly; they are primarily speech act verbs, such as *say* and *explain*, and they are commonly used to introduce indirect statements" (p. 242).

eating.' *She* **told** *him* what Mrs Gotobed <u>had asked</u> *her* to tell *him, her* exact words, and then **explained** what *she* **was** sure *she* <u>had meant</u>. Mr Evans **listened** in bulging-eyed silence, and when *he* still **didn't speak**, even when *she* <u>had finished</u>, *she* **thought** *he* <u>hadn't taken</u> it in. (Fiction)

Table 8.1 shows the descriptive statistics for both *Friends* and conversation on Biber's (1988) D1 and D2. Even though I have already addressed D1 in Chapter 4, I show it here again to emphasize the fact that *Friends* and conversation obtained very similar scores on D1, as both have high frequencies of linguistic features typifying interactive discourse (e.g., private verbs, *that*-deletion, contractions, present tense verbs, first- and second- person pronouns). From a narrative perspective, both *Friends* and conversation have a low score on D2 (*General Fiction*, for example, received a score of 6 on this continuum). However, when the 'degrees of narrativeness' are compared, conversation proves to be 3.5 times more narrative than *Friends*. It is this difference that will be explored in this chapter.

To provide a better picture of this narrative perspective, Table 8.2 below shows several registers on D2. Briefly, the closer to *romance fiction* or *general fiction* (the two most narrative registers), the more narrative the register is. In other words, the

Table 8.2 *Friends*, conversation, and selected registers on Biber's Dimension 2 (narrative vs. non-narrative discourse) (Adapted from Biber, Conrad, & Reppen (1998), p. 154)

Scores	Selected Registers
	Narrative
	Romance fiction
7	
6	General fiction
2	Biographies
0	
	Face-to-face conversation
-1	
-2	
	Friends
	Academic prose
-3	Official documents
	Broadcasts
	Non-narrative

closer to the narrative end of the continuum, the higher the frequency of past tense, third-person pronouns, perfect aspect, etc the register is likely to have. The gradual movement toward *broadcasts* (the non-narrative -- or least narrative -- end of the continuum) indicates a gradual decrease of the frequencies of these linguistic features. Therefore, the lower a register scores on this continuum, the lower the frequency of the linguistic features characterizing narrative discourse (past tense, third-person pronouns, etc) it is likely to have.

In the next section, I take a closer look at the linguistic features typifying narrative discourse. I also discuss an interesting offshoot of the frequency analysis of these features: the functionality of non-minimal responses (McCarthy, 2002) in narrative chunks of discourse.

8.2.1   The linguistic expression of narrativeness

In this section, I compare *Friends* and conversation relative to the frequency of several features: personal pronouns, past tense, perfect aspect (overall), past perfect (canonical and irrealis functions), and non-minimal responses. Non-minimal responses (e.g., *Sure*) are not usually associated with narrative discourse; I will show how they relate to narrative chunks of discourse, which are more often found in conversation. Table 8.3 shows that all of the features associated with narrative discourse present higher frequencies in conversation.

Third-person personal pronouns
I begin this analysis with third-person personal pronouns. Figure 8.1 below also includes first- and second-person pronouns to provide a better overall picture of personal pronoun use in both corpora. Not surprisingly, both corpora have much higher frequencies of first- and second-person pronouns when compared to third-person pronouns. As discussed above, high frequencies of first- and second personal pronouns are typical of involved registers.

Table 8.3 Linguistic features associated with narrative discourse

Feature	Conversation	*Friends*	Similar
Past tense	•		
3rd person pronouns	•		
Perfect aspect (overall)	•		
Past perfect (overall)	•		
Past perfect (canonical function)	•		
Non-minimal responses	•		

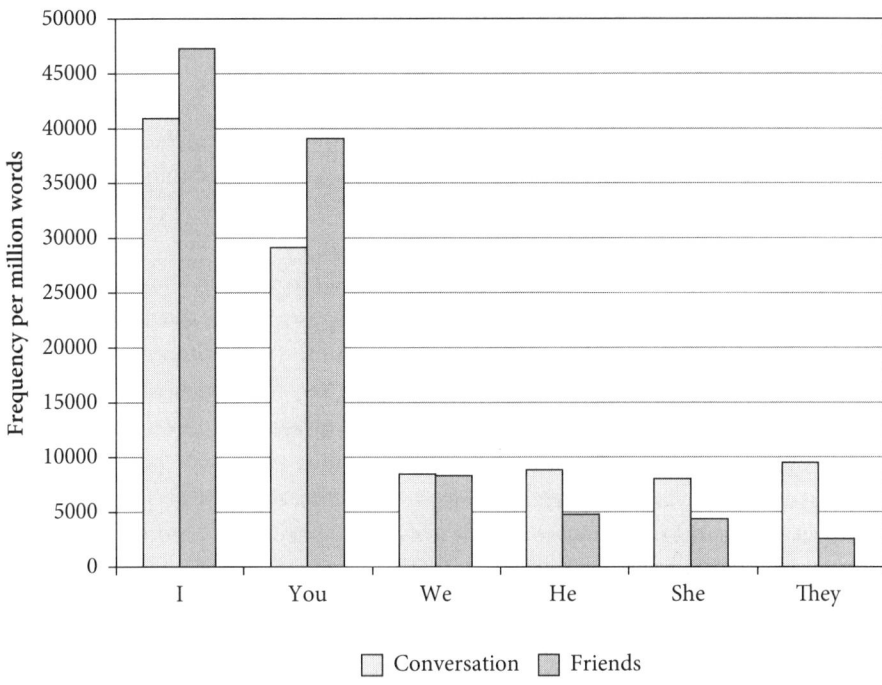

Figure 8.1 Frequency of personal pronouns in conversation and *Friends*

As Figure 8.1 reveals, the comparison of third-person personal pronoun use indicates that conversation has much higher frequencies of these pronouns. When grouped together, the frequency of third-person pronouns in conversation is over twice as high as in *Friends* (26366 instances/million words versus 11726 instances/million words in *Friends*). Further, the differences in the frequencies of first- and second-person pronouns accentuate the higher degree of narrativeness of conversation. Figure 8.1 also shows that, except for *we*, *Friends* has higher frequencies of both, first- and second- person pronouns. When grouped together, *Friends* has 94685 instances/million words of first- and second- person pronouns; in conversation they occur 78533 times/million words.

A much more striking difference, however, comes from the analysis of the proportion of first- and second-person pronouns to the number of third-person pronouns within each corpus. The ratio of first- and second-person pronouns (combined) to third-person pronouns is much higher in *Friends*: 8:1 (94685: 11726); in conversation this ratio is just 3: 1 (78533: 26366). This analysis strengthens the contrast of pronoun use in conversation and *Friends*, showing the importance of not only the *presence* of linguistic features (as revealed by higher frequencies) but also the *absence* of these features (as indicated by lower frequencies of such features).

Past tense and *perfect aspect*

Past tense and third-person pronouns are the top markers of narrative discourse (Biber, 1988). Even though third-person pronouns were discussed in the previous section, they are also included in Figure 8.2 to provide a better overall picture of the narrative dimension of conversation and *Friends*.

Past tense occurs 37310 times/million words in conversation and 29125 times/ million words in *Friends*; as described in the previous section, third-person pronouns are over 2 times more frequent in conversation. Perfect aspect is relatively rare in conversation when compared to narrative registers, such as fiction. The overall frequency of perfect aspect is higher in conversation (2591 versus 2280 instances/million words), but this difference is not as striking as past tense and third-person pronouns. The excerpt from conversation below is a typical example of narrative chunks of discourse, which are interspersed with predominantly in-volved interactions in conversation.

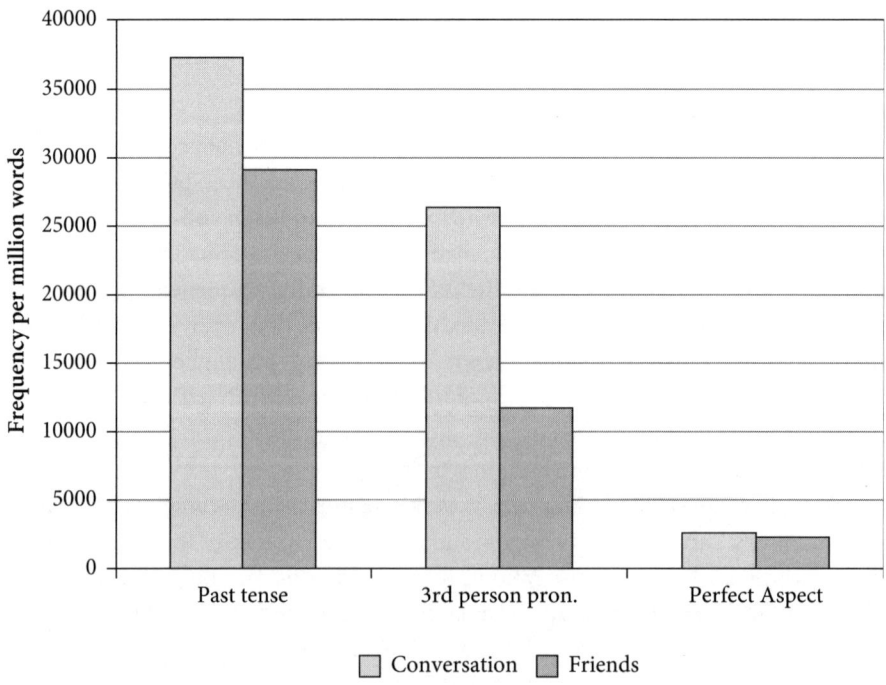

Figure 8.2 Linguistic features marking narrative discourse

1: Oh, okay. Randy's here....Bob **said** that, the... *he* would be, *they* might be a little late, *they*'ll be a little late. Uh... yeah I would encourage people to wear them under collars. Apparently the window... *he* **called** and said that the, somebody <u>**had left**</u> a window open in *his* office.

2: Uh huh.

1: And so the security people **wanted** to come down and make sure that that's what it **was**. **Was** just that somebody <u>**had left**</u> the window open.

2: Oh. (Conversation)

This short segment has six instances of past tense (in bold), five third-person pronouns (in italics), and two instances of perfect aspect (in bold, underlined). In addition, two of the past-tense verbs are public verbs (said), one of the markers of narrative discourse. Biber (1988) suggests that public verbs probably co-occur with the other markers of narrative discourse because they are often used in quotatives (indirect, reported speech).

As Biber et al. (2002) point out, "perfect aspect most often describes events or states taking place during a preceding period of time" (p. 156). The authors also show that past perfect tends to be more frequent than present perfect in fiction (which has a high degree of narrativeness) since it is "used especially for reference to an earlier period in the middle of a past tense narrative" (p. 161), as the segment above clearly illustrates: the two references to *the window that somebody <u>had left</u> open* mark an occurrence that took place before *he <u>called</u> and <u>said</u>*.

Perfect aspect breakdown
Despite the relatively low overall frequency of perfect aspect in involved registers, the analysis of past perfect adds an interesting dimension to this discussion. The breakdown of perfect aspect into present and past perfect brings further evidence of the higher degree of narrativeness inherent to conversation as compared to *Friends*. Figure 8.3 shows that past perfect is almost 3 times more frequent in conversation: it occurs 344 times/million words; in *Friends*, it occurs 119 times/million words.

Even more interesting is the breakdown of the functions of the past perfect. In its canonical function, the past perfect is a temporal marker: it is used to express time sequences, indicating the event that took place first, as in the example above. In its counterfactual function (also called irrealis or past unreal), it is used to refer to hypothetical situations: something that could happen or could have happened if the conditions were or had been different. The examples below from *Friends* and conversation illustrate this function of the past perfect:

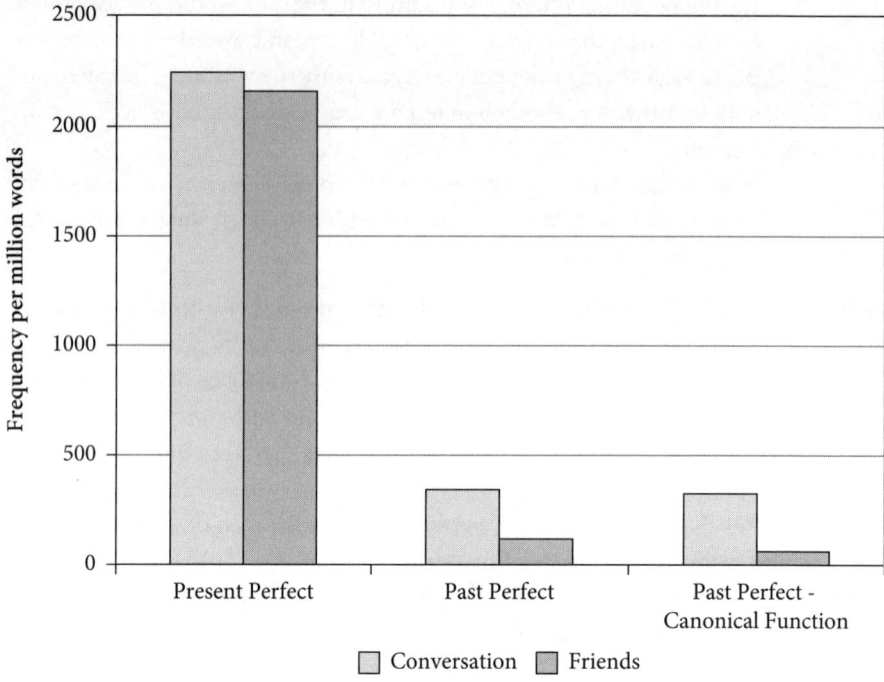

Figure 8.3 Perfect aspect breakdown in conversation and Friends

Ross: Listen, Joey, I know what he did was wrong but don't you think you could at least hear the guy out?

Joey: Back when you and Rachel were together, if Chandler **had kissed** her, would you hear him out? (*Friends*)

A: ...and that's why she couldn't see the recording levels. Well if she **had checked** she would have seen they weren't, they weren't moving.

B: They weren't moving yeah. (Conversation)

In *Friends*, the past perfect occurs with this counterfactual function in 51% of the instances: out of the total of 119 instances/million words, 61 of the occurrences refer to hypothetical situations; in conversation, of the 344 instances/million words of past perfect, only 19 instances (5.6%) occur with this function. Therefore, in conversation, not only is past perfect much more frequent overall; functionally, it is used as a marker of narrative discourse much more frequently than in *Friends*.

Non-minimal responses

Non-minimal responses, defined in Chapter 6 (Section 6.2.8), are not usually associated with narrative discourse. McCarthy (2002) points out that these single-word responses (e.g., *Yeah*) have an important communicative function in that they are indicators of attention, interest, and "good listenership" (p. 49). Figure 8.4 displays the frequency of the most common non-minimal responses in conversation and *Friends* and shows that all of them have higher frequencies in conversation.

In the extract below, there are three non-minimal responses (i.e., *yeah, mm, mm*), indicating either comprehension or interest. As in the previous extract, there are several markers of narrative discourse (third-person pronouns in italics, past tense verbs in bold, perfect aspect in bold and underlined). Interestingly, these linguistic features often co-occur with extended turns, which often have a narrative nature. This relationship between extended turns and non-minimal responses points to another characteristic that differentiates conversation from *Friends* at the discourse level: the structure of turns in conversation tends to be more "lopsided," i.e., some turns (extended turns) are much longer than others.

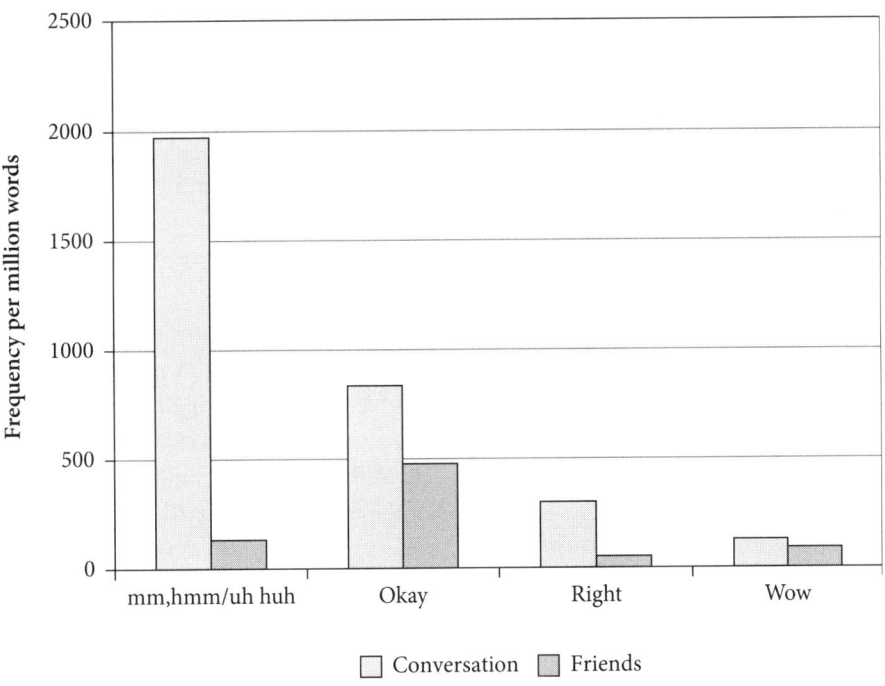

Figure 8.4 Frequency of the most common non-minimal responses in conversation and *Friends*

A: <laughing>*He, he*, you know, I couldn't understand it, all *them* big words </laughing> and I get a word here and there, [you know]

B: *[Yeah]*

A: maybe I could un=, get the drift of what *they* **were saying,** <laughing>but so funny 'cos [*they*]</laughing>

B: <laughing>Ha. I could imagine that would be</laughing>

A: **Was** kind of, I **was** glad we **went,** it was quite a, **there was** a fellow there and it **was** such a common Polish name and I can't remember it. *He* **was** from Poland and I**'d seen** when *he* **walked** in *he* **was carrying** this boy like, I would say the boy **was** six or seven years old maybe, and *he* **was carrying** *him. He* must be crippled or something. Well, then the, the fellow that's the head organist and choir is from Poland but *he's* been here for ten years or so and, uh, then *he* **said** *he's* here with *his* son, *he's* taking *him* to a, uh, Ann Arbor for surgery

B: *[Mm.]*

A: and *he* **had,** *he*, but *he* **was** going to leave 'em. I **thought,** I mean, I, you know, I'm not, those words *they* use that *they***'d use** the common words that I'm familiar, but Dorothy **said** *they* **had** to leave *him* here and *his* dad had to go back to Poland for some reason

B: [*Mm.*] (Conversation)

[] indicates overlap

8.3 The discourse immediacy of *Friends*

Discourse immediacy (see Chapter 3, Section 3.2.5.1) is characterized by exchanges that focus on immediate concerns and not on past events as in the excerpts discussed in the previous section. Speakers refer to what is happening at the moment, talk about plans for the near future, make comments or express their feelings about what is observable or happening at the moment. Linguistically, these chunks of discourse have low frequencies of the features associated with narrative discourse (e.g., past tense, third-person pronouns, perfect aspect verbs). The segment from *Friends* below starts with some 'small talk' about Rachel's dress. When Monica changes the conversation to Ross' arrival (Ross had gone to China on business), Rachel expresses her feelings about dating him and how this might negatively affect her relationship with the group of friends as a whole. This excerpt illustrates *discourse immediacy* and its characteristic focus on immediate concerns. It is interesting to notice that even when perfect aspect (*I've been thinking about it…* and *I've decided…*) is used, it prefaces an evaluative comment referring to an immediate concern: *…this whole Ross thing, it's just not a good idea.*

Monica:　　Hey, great skirt! Birthday present?
Rachel:　　Yeah.
Monica:　　Oh, from who?
Rachel:　　From you. I exchanged the blouse you got me.
Monica:　　Well, it's the thought. Hey, doesn't Ross' flight get in in a couple hours? At gate 27-B?
Rachel:　　Uh, yeah. Uh, Monica, y'know, honey, I've been thinking about it and I've decided this—this whole Ross thing, it's just not a good idea.
Monica:　　Oh, why?
Rachel:　　Because, I feel like I wouldn't just be going out with him. I would be going out with all of you. Oh, and there would just be all this pressure, and I don't wanna...
Monica:　　No, no, no, no, no, no pressure, no pressure!

[*Friends*: Season 1, episode 24 – The One Where Rachel Finds Out]

The topic of the next segment (also from *Friends*) revolves around Ross' new girl-friend and the pros and cons of the relationship. Even though this excerpt has several instances of third-person reference, it focuses on facts, evaluative comments, and immediate concerns. When the features of narrative discourse occur (e.g., six instances of third-person reference – including *she* and *her* – and past tense verbs –*did* it, *married* her, and *didn't do* that), they take on a supporting / secondary role: they occur in isolation and not as an inherent part of the set of co-occurring features performing the major discourse function of the interaction – the expression of feelings and stance. The features in bold (first- and second- person pronouns, a private verb – *mean* –, that-deletion – Ø –, present tense verbs, *do* as a pro-verb – you *did* it and I didn't *do* that –, pronoun *it*, and the general emphatic *just* reflect the involvement of the interaction.

Ross:　　　　Okay umm, bad stuff. Well, **I'm**-I'm 12 years older than she **is**.
Monica:　　If the school finds out **you**'re fired.
Ross:　　　　Hmm.
Monica:　　She's leaving for three months.
Chandler:　For camp!
Ross:　　　　Okay, good stuff. Umm, well she's-she's sweet and pretty and...
Monica:　　Look Ross, the only question Ø **you need** to ask **is**, "Do **you see** a future?" **I mean** like do **you see yourself** marrying her? (Ross pauses in consideration.) Oh my God! **You did** it already! **You** married her, didn't **you**?!

Ross: No! No! I…didn't **do** that. It's **just**… Okay, honestly no. I don't,
          I don't **see** a big future with her.

[*Friends*: Season 6, episode 24 – The One With The Proposal]

In this segment, we learn that a) Ross's girlfriend is 12 years younger than he is (fact); b) if the school finds out about the relationship (Ross was a guest lecturer at New York University, and his new girlfriend used to be his student), Ross will be fired (fact); c) the girl is leaving tomorrow (fact); d) she is "sweet and pretty" (Ross' evaluation); e) Ross did not marry her (fact); and f) he does not see a " big future" with her (fact/evaluation). Facts and evaluative statements predominate in this short excerpt; the exchanges are about an immediate concern (Ross' relationship with his new girlfriend); they are about facts and evaluations with a direct impact on what is happening at the moment.

The co-occurrence and high frequency of certain linguistic features seem to be especially characteristic of discourse immediacy. Among these are first- and second- person pronouns, vocatives (those classified as familiarizers), and greetings and leave-takings. Table 8.4 shows that virtually all of these features are more frequent in *Friends*; those that present similar counts (vocatives *folks*, *bro*, and *bud*) are extremely rare in both corpora.

Table 8.4 Linguistic features associated with discourse immediacy

Categories	Feature	Conversation	*Friends*	Similar
Personal pronouns	1st person		•	
	2nd person		•	
Vocatives (Familiarizers)	Guys		•	
	Man		•	
	Dude		•	
	Buddy		•	
	Folks			•
	Bro			•
	Bud			•
Overall greetings & leave-takings			•	

Personal pronouns

In Section 8.2.1, I discussed the use of personal pronouns and showed that *Friends* has a higher frequency of first- and second-person pronouns. In addition, the ratio of first- and second-person pronouns (combined) to third-person pronouns is 8 times higher in *Friends*, thus underscoring this difference between the two corpora: the higher frequency of first- and second-person pronouns is accentuated by the lower frequency of third-person pronouns. At the discourse level, such a difference translates into exchanges focusing on immediate concerns, as in the segment below:

Ross:	**You** still love **me**?
Rachel:	No.
Ross:	**You** still love **me**.
Rachel:	Oh, y-yeah, so, **you-you** love **me**!
Ross:	No, nnnnn. What does this mean? What do **you**, I mean do **you** wanna get back together?
Rachel:	No! Maybe! **I**, **I** don't know. Ross, **I** still can't forgive **you** for what **you** did, **I** can't, **I** just, but sometimes when **I**'m with **you** **I** just, **I** feel so... (*Friends*)

[*Friends*: Season 3, episode 25- The One At The Beach]

Vocatives (familiarizers), greetings, and leave-takings

Vocatives (familizarizers), greetings, and leave-takings were discussed in Chapter 7 (Sections 7.2.3–4) as markers of informality. The most frequent familiarizers in both corpora are *guys*, *man*, and *dude*; *hi* and *hey* are the most frequent greeting forms; and *bye* and *bye-bye* are the most common leave-takings.

Figure 8.5 below shows that the frequency of these features is much higher in *Friends*. Overall, vocatives are 3.5 times more frequent in *Friends* occurring 2657 times/million words; in conversation they occur 767 times/million. Greetings are 10 times more frequent in *Friends* with 3297 instances/million words versus 328 instances/million words in conversation. The difference in the number of leave-takings is less striking: *Friends* has only twice as many, 529 instances/million words versus 259 instances/million words in conversation.

Familiarizers are naturally associated with first- and second-person pronouns as they directly refer to the interlocutor and thus co-occur very frequently. The enormous disparity in the frequency of greetings is related to situational factors. *Friends* has several scenes in which the characters arrive (especially) and leave. The conversation corpus does not capture this natural characteristic of interactions due to technical limitations: conversations are usually recorded in particular places without much 'movement' of speakers. In other words, speakers do not keep arriving and leaving as frequently as in the television show. Even though this

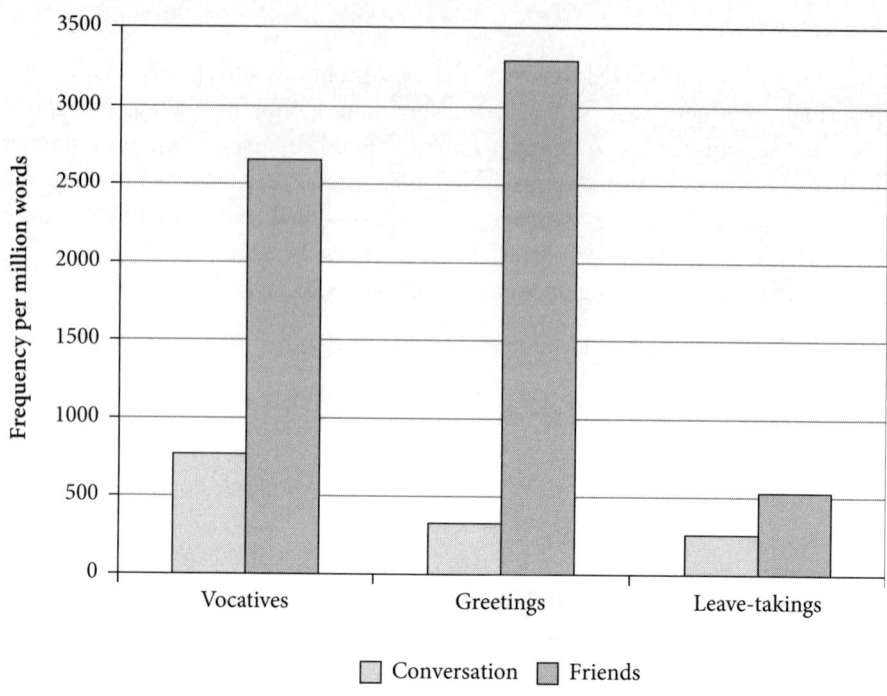

Figure 8.5 Combined frequencies of the most common vocatives, greetings, and leave-takings in conversation and *Friends*

difference is merely situational, it does add to the overall discourse immediacy of *Friends*. In the excerpt below, *guys* co-occurs with *hey*, *hi*, eight instances of *I* and two of *you*.

Rachel:	**Hey... Hi** you **guys!** Listen, **you** know what? I'm not feeling really well. I think I can't get out for the play.
Ross:	Really? Wh-what's wrong?
Rachel:	I don't know! I think it's kind of serious! Oh, **you** know... I was watching this thing on TV this morning about... Newcastle disease... and I think I might have it!!

[Season 9, episode 20: The One With The Soap Opera Party]

8.4 Summary

In this chapter, I pointed out that registers should be analyzed from different perspectives. Despite the striking similarities between *Friends* and natural conversation from an involved standpoint, the two registers show considerable differences in their degrees of narrativeness. Overall, conversation is characterized by higher frequencies of linguistic features associated with narrative discourse.

In his discussion of narrative discourse, Biber (1988) refers to past tense and third-person pronouns stating that "narrative discourse depends heavily on these two features, presenting a sequential description of past events involving specific animate participants" (p. 109). Even though differences in the frequencies of these features are the most striking differentiating factors on the narrative continuum, other features add to this difference. Despite the overall low frequency of perfect aspect in both corpora (in comparison to predominantly narrative registers), past perfect in its canonical function proved to be much more common in conversation. At the discourse level, I showed how non-minimal responses relate to narrative chunks of discourse. The common co-occurrence of these single-word responses and extended turns revealed another interesting difference: the higher frequency of lop-sided turns in conversation, which are not usually frequent in television dialogue. Finally, a much higher ratio of first- and second-person pronouns to third-person pronouns along with higher frequencies of vocatives (familiarizers), and greetings and leave-takings show that *Friends* tends to be characterized by a discourse immediacy, with its focus on immediate concerns, facts, and evaluative utterances.

CHAPTER 9

That's a wrap

Implications and applications

Much of the discussion presented in the preceding chapters was based on the results reported in Biber's (1988) study of English register variation and in LGSWE. In fact, the surprising similarities between *Friends* and natural conversation revealed by the multidimensional analysis were the motivation for the second phase of the present study, which focused on functional differences between the two corpora.

The analysis of *Friends* was carried out through a comparison to naturally-occurring conversation. As a natural offshoot of this research design, the present study provides a comprehensive description of many of the most common linguistic features that characterize natural conversation. As I pointed out throughout the book, *Friends* presents high frequencies of the vast majority of features typifying conversation. When these linguistic features and their functional correlates are more closely studied, important differences emerge from this analysis; these differences ultimately characterize each of the corpora.

In this concluding chapter, I provide a summary of the major findings of the present study:

1. *Friends* shares the core linguistic features that characterize natural conversation;
2. Vague language is much more pervasive in natural conversation than in *Friends*;
3. *Friends* presents higher frequencies of linguistic features marking emotional language;
4. *Friends* presents higher frequencies of linguistic features marking informality;
5. Natural conversation has a higher degree of narrativeness when compared to *Friends*;
6. Some differences between the two corpora are due to restrictions and/or influences of the televised medium.

In the following sections, each of these findings is addressed.

9.1 Linguistic similarities

Biber's (1988) study of English register variation concluded that registers are characterized by high frequencies of specific sets of co-occurring linguistic features. These features tend to co-occur because they perform similar functions. Biber's Dimension 1 (D1), *involved versus informational production*, reveals a continuum ranging from highly involved (interactive) to highly informational registers. Highly involved registers, like face-to-face conversation, tend to present high frequencies of features, such as private/mental verbs, *that*-deletion, contractions, present-tense verbs, and first- and second-person personal pronouns. Conversely, highly informational registers, like academic prose, tend to be characterized by high frequencies of features, such as nouns, nominalizations, prepositions, attributive adjectives, and agent-less passive constructions. The first group of features ('positive features') and the second group of features ('negative features') are said to be in complementary distribution: registers characterized by high frequencies of the positive features tend to have very low frequencies of the negative features and vice versa.

The multidimensional analysis of *Friends* yielded a score of 34.4 on D1 (face-to-face conversation scored 35.3 on D1), revealing that *Friends* shares the core linguistic features that characterize involved registers, such as conversation. The short excerpt from *Friends* below illustrates some of Biber's D1 features: among other conversational features, it has several instances of first- and second- person pronouns (underlined), contractions (bold), and private/mental verbs (italics). Table 9.1 shows where *Friends* plots on D1 along with other selected registers.

(1) Rachel: Hey... Hi you guys! Listen, you *know* what? **I'm** not *feeling* really well. I *think* I **can't** get out for the play.

Ross: Really? Wh-what's wrong?

Rachel: I **don't** *know*! I *think* **it's** kind of serious! Oh, you know... I was watching this thing on TV this morning about... Newcastle disease... and I *think* I might have it!! (*Friends*)

Despite the striking linguistic similarities, the multidimensional analysis also revealed that conversation presents much more variation than *Friends*, as attested by the standard deviation values (9.1 in conversation vs. 4.3 in *Friends*). This disparity is most likely attributed to the much narrower range of settings, interaction types, and topics in *Friends* (discussed in Chapter 3).

Table 9.1 *Friends* on Biber's D1 along with selected registers

Scores	Selected registers
	Involved
	Telephone conversations
35	**Face-to-face conversation**
	Friends
20	Personal letters
5	
	Prepared speeches
0	
	General Fiction
-10	Press editorials
-15	Academic prose
	Official documents
	Informational

9.2 Vague language

The shared context in which face-to-face conversation takes place and the pressures of online production lead speakers to make frequent use of 'vague linguistic devices,' such as hedges (e.g., *kind of*), nouns of vague reference (e.g., *stuff*), and vague coordination tags (e.g., *or something*). These vague devices perform important discourse functions at different levels:

a. The "strategic imprecision" (Leech, 2000, p. 695) resulting from their use allows speakers to speed up the communicative process as well as share the construction of meaning. In example (2), speaker A shows his awareness of the inaccuracy of his word choice: *honorary degree*. The apparent imprecision that *sort of honorary degree* confers to the utterance is strategic in that it 'frees' speaker A of the need to elaborate on the explanation, which would be likely to truncate the communicative exchange. The overall *idea* provided by *sort of honorary degree* allows speaker B to actively participate in the communicative event as he is, in a sense, 'invited' to share the construction of meaning with his interlocutor. Further, should the utterance prove to be too vague to understand, interlocutors can resort to clarification questions, which ultimately contribute to keeping the communicative process dynamic and interactive.

> (2)   A: and, uh, he showed them to some university professors at UNM or someone did and now <unclear> he's got some <u>sort of</u> honorary degree.
>
>   B: I think they, they gave him permission to go fossil hunting in places where only university folks can go. (Conversation)

b. Vague devices can also mitigate the potential negative impact that an overly direct utterance might have. The vague coordination tag in (3), *or something*, translates into flexibility on the part of the speaker, showing his attempt to not impose on the interlocutor.

> (3)   Richard: So, you wanna get a hamburger <u>or something</u>?
>
>   Monica: Oh, um, I don't know if that's a good idea.
>
>   Richard: Oh. Look, just friends, I won't grope you. I promise. (*Friends*)

In addition to these more obvious vague devices, I have shown that linguistic features, such as modals *could* and *might*, discourse markers *you know* and *I mean*, stance markers *probably*, *perhaps*, and *maybe*, copular verbs *seem* and *appear* can also be instrumental in the expression of vagueness. Despite the fact that, overall, *Friends* has high frequencies of vague devices, most of these features have higher frequencies in conversation. Conversation has thus been shown to be typically more vague than the dialogues in *Friends*. Some of the possible reasons for this difference are addressed in Section 9.6, below.

9.3   Emotional language

Speakers use language for a wide range of communicative purposes: in addition to conveying information, speakers express opinions, feelings, and attitudes. Emphatic content and emotions are reflected not only in the speakers' tone of voice, intonation patterns, and nonverbal devices, such as gestures and facial expression; when speakers express emotional content, they make specific choices of linguistic features. Emotional content is expressed through the use of numerous linguistic features, such as adverbial intensifiers (e.g., *so*), certain discourse markers (e.g., *wow*), some expletives (e.g., *damn*), certain lexical bundles (e.g., *I can't believe* + complements), emphatic *do*, some slang terms (e.g., *freak out*), and even by the 'sensory copular verbs' (LGSWE, p. 442), *look*, *feel*, and *sound*.

Of the 32 features associated with emotional language selected for analysis, only three were more frequent in conversation, including the expletives *shit* and *fuck*, which are absent in the *Friends* data due to restrictions imposed by the television network (discussed in Section 9.6). Surprisingly, all of the other expletives selected for analysis were considerably more frequent in *Friends*, including *damn*, *bitch*, *son of a bitch*, and *crap*. Example (4) from *Friends* exemplifies some of these features, showing how they collaboratively co-occur in the expression of emotion.

(4) Rachel: You <u>really</u> think I didn't say goodbye to you because I don't care?
     Ross: That's what it seemed like.
     Rachel: <u>I cannot believe</u> that after ten years, you do not know ONE thing about me.
     Ross: <u>Fine</u>, then why didn't you say something?
     Rachel: Because it is <u>too</u> <u>damn</u> hard Ross. I can't even begin to explain to you how much I'm gonna miss you. (*Friends*)

It should be noted that some linguistic features may have different functions in different contexts or even perform multiple functions in the same context. For example, *totally*, as in (5), is a linguistic innovation of American English conversation. Similar to *absolutely*, in this context *totally* expresses emphatic agreement and, by virtue of its semantic nature, naturally expresses emphatic content. The same *totally* is also analyzed as a marker of informality in Chapter 7. This 'double-dipping' should not be seen as repetitive; rather, it is a natural reflection of the interactive nature of conversation.

(5) Chandler: That's a great idea! We can easily think of a way for us both to enjoy the room.
     Monica: <u>Totally!</u> (*Friends*)

9.4 Informal language

The multidimensional analysis (Biber, 1988) of *Friends* was focused on Biber's D1, *involved vs. informational production*. Briefly, 'texts' that score high on D1 have high frequencies of the features that typify interactive registers. As such, involvement is linguistically realized by features, such as private verbs, contractions, first- and second-person pronouns, etc (as summarized in Section 9.1). The analysis revealed that *Friends* shares the core linguistic features of involved registers.

The second phase of the present study included a frequency-based comparison of a large number of linguistic features associated with informal language. These markers of informality included features, such as expletives (e.g., *son of a bitch*), slang terms (e.g., *cool*), and some linguistic innovations (e.g., preposition

IN in negative statements with present perfect aspect followed by a time expression, as in *I haven't seen you in ages.*). Similar to emotional language, *Friends* consistently presented higher frequencies of most of these features. Of the 35 features selected for analysis, 31 were more frequent in *Friends*; only three of these features were more frequent in conversation: expletives *shit* and *fuck* + variations (which are absent in *Friends*) and the borderline slang term/expletive *pissed* (*off*).

As I commented in the previous section, some linguistic features may perform more than one function. For this reason, some of the features (e.g., expletives, slang) were included in both analyses (emotional and informal language). Slang terms, overall, are markers of informality. Due to their semantic nature, some seem to be more clearly associated with emotional language (e.g., *damn*); others, such as *What's up?* (used as a greeting), do not seem to reflect emphatic content. Since the conversation corpus is not annotated for prosodic patterns, it is not always clear if the primary function of the feature is to convey emotion or informality. Because of this 'hybrid nature,' most expletives and slang terms were analyzed both as markers of informality and emotional language.

Overall, it seems that scriptwriters and actors deliberately tried to portray the language of the show as informal, which is appropriate when the types of social relationships shared by the characters are taken into account. However, the excessive informality revealed by the analysis suggests a case of hypercorrection: in the attempt to make the language of *Friends* 'very' informal, scriptwriters and actors might have 'overshot the colloquial mark.' However, it seems plausible to argue that this overly informal linguistic environment may reflect the extremely casual and intimate social relationships shared by the characters in the show. Had the conversation corpus reflected a similar social context, these marked differences might not have been as striking.

In addition to certain informal lexical choices (e.g., *dude*, *guy*, *wow*), the segment from *Friends* that concludes this section illustrates how the involved features of Biber's D1 (discussed in Chapter 4) interact with the additional features associated with the discourse circumstances of conversation, discussed in LGSWE (Chapter 14, *The Grammar of Conversation*) and in Chapter 7 of this book. All of these features collaboratively support the intended discourse purposes of the exchanges. The linguistic features of Biber's D1 are italicized and labeled in curly brackets; the additional markers of informality discussed in Chapter 7 are underlined and labeled in square brackets.

> Ross: <u>Dude</u> [vocative/familiarizer], we are <u>so</u> [innovation] <u>gonna</u> [contracted semi-modal] party!
>
> Phoebe: Wow! Okay, dude alert! And who *is* {be as main verb} this guy?

Ross: Mike "Gandolf" Ganderson, only like the funest guy in the world.

Chandler: I'*m* {contraction} <u>gonna</u> [contracted semi-modal] call and get off work tomorrow!

Ross: I'*m* {contraction} <u>gonna</u> [contracted semi-modal] call after you!

Chandler: *This* {demonstrative pronoun} is <u>gonna</u> [contracted semi-modal] be so <u>cool</u> [slang], <u>dude</u>, [vocative/familiarizer], we never party anymore!

[*Friends*: Season 4, episode 9 – The One Where They're Gonna Party]

9.5 Degrees of narrativeness

For registers to be more fully understood, they should be considered from a multidimensional standpoint. Despite the striking similarities between *Friends* and conversation on Biber's D1, the two registers present considerable differences in their degrees of narrativeness. Linguistic features associated with narrative discourse (e.g., past tense verbs, third-person pronouns, perfect aspect, public verbs) are, overall, considerably more frequent in conversation. In other words, despite the low degrees of narrativeness in both corpora when compared to typically narrative registers, such as fiction, the predominantly involved exchanges found in conversation are more often interspersed with narrative chunks of discourse when compared to *Friends*.

When perfect aspect is broken down into present and past perfect, interesting differences emerge from the analysis. Despite the overall low and similar frequencies of perfect aspect in both corpora (as compared to narrative registers), past perfect proved to be three times more frequent in conversation. Further, the breakdown of past perfect into its canonical and counterfactual functions accentuates this difference. In its canonical function, past perfect is a temporal marker, indicating the sequence in which past events take place, as in (6). With this function, past perfect occurs approximately 95% of the time in conversation.

(6) A: When we first got in like a long time ago and you <u>had</u> just <u>ridden</u> in it, who the hell is this little skinny person?

     B: <nv_laugh>

     A: He had to let it out all the way. (Conversation)

The analysis of narrativeness also revealed an interesting peculiarity: narrative chunks of discourse often co-occur with non-minimal responses (McCarthy,

2002) (e.g., *sure*, *right*, *okay*): one of the speakers produces an extended turn; the other responds with these single-word utterances, which function as indicators of interest, understanding, or as McCarthy (2002) puts it, "good listenership." This type of interaction causes the structure of turns to become uneven, as in (7). This turn structure is not desirable in *Friends* and is addressed in Section 9.6.

(7)   A: Was kind of, I was glad we went, it was quite a, there was a fellow there and it was such a common Polish name and I can't remember it. He was from Poland and I'd seen when he walked in he was carrying this boy like, I would say the boy was six or seven years old maybe, and he was carrying him. He must be crippled or something. Well, then the, the fellow that's the head organist and choir is from Poland but he's been here for ten years or so and, uh, then he said he's here with his son, he's taking him to a, uh, Ann Arbor for surgery

      B: <u>Mm</u>.

      A: and he had, he, but he was going to leave 'em. I thought, I mean, I, you know, I'm not, those words they use that they'd use the common words that I'm familiar, but Dorothy said they had to leave him here and his dad had to go back to Poland for some reason

      B: <u>Mm</u>. (Conversation)

In relative terms, just like conversation tends to more constantly present narrative chunks of discourse, *Friends* is predominantly characterized by discourse immediacy. Discourse immediacy – similar to what Chafe (1994) calls 'immediate mode' – refers to a focus on immediate concerns, as opposed to the recount of past events which do not directly impact what is happening at the present moment or will happen in the near future. At the discourse level, this functional characteristic is reflected in the turn structure, which, unlike in natural conversation, tends to be more evenly distributed. Features, such as first- and second-person pronouns, vocatives, and greetings and leave-takings tend to be associated with the discourse immediacy of *Friends*. Just like past perfect with its canonical function adds to the narrativeness of conversation, its counterfactual function, as in (8), helps to shape the discourse immediacy of *Friends*.

(8)   Chandler: Yeah, I just ordered a beer!
      Waiter: You're straight. I get it.
      Monica: I still say that if we <u>had called</u> your dad we could've gotten better seats.

9.6 Restrictions and/or influences of the televised medium

Some of the potential differences between *Friends* and conversation seem to result from either restrictions imposed by the televised medium, overall, and/or the television network, in particular, or the nature of this particular show. For example, the analysis of emotional and informal language involved the use of expletives. Despite the surprisingly higher overall frequency of expletives in *Friends*, the two most frequent expletives in natural conversation, *shit* and *fuck* (+ *variations*), are absent in the *Friends* data. This 'linguistic absence' is obviously not just a coincidence; regardless of the authorship of this decision, it adds to the differences between the two corpora. It should be noted that I am by no means advocating the use of expletives in prime-time television; rather, I am pointing out a linguistic element that contributes to differentiating *Friends* from conversation.

The analysis of vague language showed that conversation makes much more frequent use of vague linguistic devices (e.g., hedges, nouns of vague reference, vague coordination tags) than *Friends*. Shared context and the 'nature' of the interlocutors in the two corpora can help us understand the potential reasons for this discrepancy in frequency counts. Casual conversation is much more likely to take place in shared context. This way, elaboration of meaning is undesirable and may, in fact, disrupt the flow of communication. The apparent imprecision brought about by vague language may actually speed up the communicative process, thus adding to the dynamic nature of conversational interactions as interlocutors actively contribute to the co-construction of meaning. The interlocutors in *Friends* are obviously not restricted to the characters themselves; rather, the 'real interlocutors' are millions of spectators who must at least minimally share the context in which exchanges take place. It seems plausible to conclude that the use of vague devices in *Friends* is delimited by a 'linguistic boundary' beyond which comprehension is hindered.

The analysis of degrees of narrativeness showed that narrative chunks of discourse tend to co-occur with non-minimal responses, discussed in Section 9.5 above. This peculiarity gives rise to extended turns and a lopsided turn structure. The uneven allocation of time ends up giving much,more exposure to individual characters and, potentially, making the 'temporary monologue' harder to follow and dialogues less dynamic overall. On the other hand, the discourse immediacy that characterizes the verbal exchanges in *Friends* contributes to the cinematic and interactive nature of television in general.

Though it is beyond the scope of the present study, it should be noted that humor may have a direct influence on the choice of linguistic features made by scriptwriters. Much of the humor in *Friends* is created through pragmatic failure. As such, the *unexpected* is often linguistically realized by *unexpected* linguistic choices. For example, overly emotional or informal utterances with the purpose of 'adding humor' to dialogues may have been responsible for the higher frequencies of features marking emotional or informal language. The addition of humor can also attribute unexpected functions to certain linguistic features. For example, the co-occurrence of vague linguistic devices (meant to avoid elaboration of meaning and speed up the communicative process) with overly elaborated explanations may render the choice of features linguistically inappropriate or unnecessary but highly effective for the purpose of creating humor. Excerpt (9) illustrates this apparent structural-functional mismatch: the hedge *sort of* is paradoxically followed by a clear instance of elaboration of meaning.

> (9)   Monica: I hate men! I hate men!
> Phoebe: Oh no, don't hate, you don't want to put that out into the universe.
> Monica: Is it me? Is it like I have some *sort of* beacon that only dogs and men with severe emotional problems can hear? (*Friends*)

Finally, the situational circumstances of *Friends* should not be overlooked. On the one hand, the intimate relationships shared by the characters may have led the features marking emotional content and informality to be much more prevalent in *Friends*. It is plausible to assume that the differences between the two corpora would not have been so striking had the conversation corpus captured the full range of interactions in similar contexts. On the other hand, features such as greetings and leave-takings as well as vocatives (familiarizers) would not have presented such disparity in frequency counts had the conversation corpus more frequently captured all of those moments when speakers meet, as is the case of many scenes in *Friends*, which open with the characters meeting in one of the characters' apartments or at *Central Perk*, the coffee house where the *friends* often 'hang out.'

9.7 Implications and applications

The present study has shown that *Friends* shares the core linguistic features that characterize involved registers, such as face-to-face conversation. As I pointed out throughout the book, this does not mean that the scripted language of *Friends* is the same as natural conversation. Several differences were explored in the preceding chapters; others, such as the virtual absence of overlaps and interruptions, as well as differences related to pragmatics were acknowledged but are beyond the scope of this study.

Once the differences are acknowledged, the numerous similarities can be explored for different purposes. For example, the use of television dialogue as a surrogate for natural conversation for the analysis of certain linguistic features seems perfectly appropriate. As Rey (2001) has noted, the language of television dialogue is a reflection of the perception that scriptwriters (and actors) have of actual conversation. As such, the analysis of certain features –especially those that are less likely to be captured by a corpus of natural conversation -- could be based on television dialogue. Further, a corpus of 'dialogues' that spans over a period of ten years is extremely hard to come by. *Friends* as well as many other television shows have the potential of providing extremely interesting data for diachronic studies, especially those focusing on lexico-grammatical features. Though not the focus of the present study, processes of language change in progress, such as the use of the adverbial intensifier *so* modifying features other than adjectives and adverbs, as well as the innovative uses of *totally* in American English conversation were fully captured in the *Friends* corpus.

Television dialogue also offers a vast potential for pedagogical purposes. The increasing availability of DVDs of recent television shows can provide fairly accurate examples of the relationship between certain structural forms and their functional correlates for ESL (English as a Second Language) purposes. Provided that potential differences are acknowledged by instructors, numerous examples of features that characterize natural conversation can be illustrated with a television show such as *Friends*. As I pointed out throughout the book, the vast majority of the conversational features analyzed in the present study can be found in *Friends*. For example, despite the pronounced differences in frequency counts (and perhaps some idiosyncratic uses) of vague linguistic devices, *Friends* has numerous adequate examples of vague language for ESL purposes.

The differences between natural conversation and television dialogue can also be explored for conversation studies. For example, by comparing the use of certain linguistic features in the two registers, graduate students as well as researchers can become more aware of the characteristics of natural conversation. In this sense, television studies can contribute to our understanding of the intricacies of natural conversation.

Finally, television dialogue can be explored as an object of study in itself. The study of the language of situation comedies, for example, can help us better understand the linguistic realization of humor. Several other genres of television dialogue are also readily available for linguistic studies and can further our understanding not only of individual television genres but of natural conversation as well.

9.8 Final remarks

The findings of the present study are limited to *Friends* and should not be generalized to other situation comedies or to television dialogue in general. However, I believe this study strongly indicates that television dialogue has much potential to provide us with important data for linguistic analysis. I hope that the *Friends study* will encourage other researchers to devote more attention to this virtually unexplored, yet exciting research area.

References

Adams, M. (2000). Ephemeral language. *American Speech 75*(4), 382–384.

Adoni, H., Cohen, A. A., & Mane, S. (1984). Adolescents' perception of social conflicts in social reality and television news. *Journal of Broadcasting, 28*, 33–49.

Aijmer, K. (1984). *Sort of* and *kind of* in English conversation. *Studia Linguistica, 38*, 118–128.

Aijmer, K. (1987). *Oh* and *Ah* in English conversation. *Costerus 59*, 61–86.

Aijmer, K. (1996). *Conversational routines in English: Convention and creativity.* New York, NY: Longman.

Aijmer, K. (2002). *English discourse particles: Evidence from a corpus.* Amsterdam: John Benjamins.

Altenberg, B. (1998). On the phraseology of spoken English: The evidence of recurrent word combinations. In A. P. Cowie (Ed.), *Phraseology* (pp. 101–122). Oxford: Oxford University Press.

Andersen, G. (2000). *Pragmatic markers and sociolinguistic variation: A relevance-theoretic approach to the language of adolescents.* Amsterdam/Philadelphia: John Benjamins.

Arndt, H., & Janney, R. W. (1991). Verbal, prosodic, and kinesic emotive contrasts in speech. *Journal of Pragmatics, 15*, 521–549.

Banerjee, S., & Pedersen, T. (2003). The design, implementation, and use of the Ngram Statistics Package. *Lecture Notes in Computer Science, Vol 2588*, 370–381.

Bargiela-Chiappini, F. (2003). Face and politeness: new (insights) for old (concepts). *Journal of Pragmatics, 35*,1453–1469.

Barlow, M. (2002). MonoConc Pro, version 2.2 [computer software]. Houston, TX: Athelstan. (Available at http://www.athel.com)

Battles, K., & Morrow-Hilton, W. (2002). Gay characters in conventional spaces: Will and Grace and the situation comedy genre. *Critical Studies in Media Communication, 19*(1), 87–105.

Bernan, R. (1987). *How television sees its audience: A look at the looking glass.* Newbury Park, CA: Sage Publications.

Biber (1988). *Variation across speech and writing.* Cambridge: Cambridge University Press.

Biber, D., & Conrad S. (2001). Quantitative corpus-based research: Much more than bean counting. *TESOL Quarterly, 35*, 331–336.

Biber, D., Conrad, S., & Reppen R. (1998). *Corpus linguistics: Investigating language structure and use.* New York, NY: Cambridge University Press.

Biber, D., Conrad, S., & Leech, G. (2002). *Longman student grammar of spoken and written English.* Harlow, Essex: Longman.

Biber, D., Conrad, S., & Cortes, V. (2004). *If you look at…*: Lexical bundles in university teaching and textbooks. *Applied Linguistics 25*, 371–405.

Biber, D., Johansson, S., Leech, G., Conrad, S., & Finegan, E. (1999). *Longman grammar of spoken and written English.* London: Longman.

Biber, D., Conrad, S., Reppen, R., Byrd, P., & Helt, M. (2002). Speaking and writing in the university: A multidimensional comparison. *TESOL Quarterly, 36*, 9–48.

Bright, K.S., Kauffman, M., & Crane D. (Executive Producers). (1994). *Friends* [Television series], New York, National Broadcasting Company.

Caffi, C., & Janney R. W. (1994). Towards a pragmatics of emotive communication. *Journal of Pragmatics, 22*, 325–73.

Carter, R. (2003). The grammar of talk: Spoken English, grammar and the classroom. In *Qualifications and Curriculum Authority*. London.

Carter, R., & McCarthy, M. (2006). *Cambridge grammar of English*. Cambridge: Cambridge University Press.

Chafe, W. (1994). *Discourse, consciousness and time*. Chicago: The University of Chicago Press.

Channell, J. M. (1994) *Vague language*. Oxford: Oxford University Press.

Cohen, A. A., Adoni, H., & Bantz, C. R. (1990). *Social conflict and television news*. Newbury Park, CA: Sage Publications.

Conner-Linton, J. (1989). *Crosstalk: A multi-feature analysis of Soviet-American spacebridges*. Unpublished Doctoral Dissertation: University of Southern California.

Conrad, S. (2001). Variation among disciplinary texts: A comparison of textbooks and journal articles in biology and history. In S. Conrad & D. Biber (Eds.), *Variation in English: Multi-dimensional studies* (pp. 94–107). London: Longman.

Conrad, S., & Biber, D. (2000). Adverbial marking of stance in speech and writing. In S. Hunston & G. Thompson (Eds.), *Evaluation in text: Authorial stance and the construction of discourse* (pp. 56–73). Oxford: Oxford University Press.

Conrad, S., & Biber, D. (2001). *Variation in English: Multi-dimensional studies*. London: Longman.

Cooper, D. (1997). *Writing great screenplays for film and television*. Lawrenceville, NY: ARCO.

Cooper, T. C. (2001). "Does is suck?" Or "is it for the birds?" Native speaker judgment of slang expressions. *American Speech, 76*, 62–78.

Cortes, V. (2004). Lexical bundles in published and student disciplinary writing: Examples from history and biology. *English for Specific Purposes, 23*, 397–423.

Cotterill, J. (2007). 'I think he was kind of shouting or something': Uses and abuses of vagueness in the British courtroom. In J. Cutting (Ed.), *Vague language explored* (pp. 97–114). Basingstoke: Palgrave Macmillan.

Coulmas, F. (Ed.) (1981). *Conversational routine: Explorations in standardized communication situations and prepatterned speech*. The Hague: Mouton.

Cutting, J. (2007). *Vague Language explored*. London: Palgrave.

Davis, S., & Mares, M. (1998). Effects of talk show viewing on adolescents. *Journal of Communication, 48*(3), 69–86.

Dimaggio, M. (1990). *How to write for television*. New York, NY: Fireside Publishers.

DuBois, S. (1993). Extension particles, etc. *Language Variation and Change, 4*, 179–203.

Dunning, T. (1993). Accurate methods for the statistics of surprise and coincidence. *Computational Linguistics, 19*(1), 61–74.

Erman, B. (1986). Some pragmatic expressions in English conversation. In G. Tottie & I. Backlund (Eds.), *English in speech and writing: A symposium* (pp. 131–147). Studia Anglistica Upsaliensia 60, Stockholm: Almqvist & Wiksell.

Evison, J., McCarthy, M., & O'Keeffe, A. (2007). 'Looking out for love and all the rest of it': Vague category markers as shared social space. In J. Cutting (Ed.), *Vague language explored* (pp. 138–157). Basingstoke: Palgrave Macmillan.

Fiske, J. (1987). *Television culture*. London: Methuen.

Fitzmaurice, S. (2000). "The great leveler: The role of the spoken media in stylistic shift from the colloquial to the conventional. *American Speech, 75*, 54–68.

Ford, C. E., Fox, B. A., & Thompson, S. A. (2002). *The language of turn and sequence.* New York, NY: Oxford University Press.

Fuller, J. M. (2003). The influence of speaker roles on discourse marker use. *Journal of Pragmatics, 35*, 23–45.

Grabe, M. E. (2002). Maintaining the moral order: A functional analysis of "The Jerry Springer Show." *Critical Studies in Media Communication, 19*(3), 311–328.

Grice, H. P. (1975). Logic and conversation. In P. Cole & J. Morgan (Eds.), *Speech acts, Vol. 3 of syntax and semantics* (pp. 41–58). New York, NY: Academic Press.

Grice, H. P. (1989). *Studies in the way of words.* Cambridge, MA: Harvard University Press.

Haarman, L. (2001). Performing talk. In A. Tolson (Ed.), *Television talk shows: Discourse, performance, spectacle* (pp. 31–64). Mahwah, NJ: Lawrence Erlbaum.

Helt, M. E. (2001). A multi-dimensional comparison of British and American spoken English. In S. Conrad & D. Biber (Eds.), *Variation in English: Multi-dimensional studies* (pp. 171–183). London: Longman.

Horton, A. (1999). *Writing the character-centered screenplay.* Los Angeles, CA: University of California Press.

Hunter, L. (1994). *Lew Hunter's screenwriting 434.* New York, NY: Berkeley Publishing Group.

Jucker, A. H., & Smith, S. W. (1998). And people just you know like 'wow': Discourse markers as negotiating strategies. In A. H. Jucker & Z. Yael (Eds.), *Discourse markers: Descriptions and theory* (pp. 171–201). Amsterdam: John Benjamins.

Jucker, A. H., Smith, S. W., & Lüdge, T. (2003). Interactive aspects of vagueness in conversation. *Journal of Pragmatics, 35*, 1737–1769.

Kaye, B. K., & Sapolsky, B. S. (2001). Offensive language in prime time television: Before and after content ratings. *Journal of Broadcasting & Electronic Media, 45*(2), 303–319.

Leech, G. (1999). The distribution and function of vocatives in American and British English conversation. In H. Hasselgard & S. Oksefjell (Eds), *Out of corpora: Studies in honour of Stig Johansson* (pp. 107–118). Amsterdam: Rodopi.

Leech, G. (2000). Grammars of spoken English: New outcomes of corpus-oriented research. *Language Learning, 50(4)*, 675–724.

Lembo, R. (2000). *Thinking through television.* Cambridge: Cambridge University Press.

LGSWE – see Biber et al. (1999).

McCarthy, M. (1998). *Spoken language & applied linguistics.* Cambridge: Cambridge University Press.

McCarthy, M. (2002). Good listenership made plain: British and American non-minimal response tokens in everyday conversation. In R. Reppen, S. Fitzmaurice, & D. Biber (Eds.), *Using corpora to explore linguistic variation* (pp. 49–71). Amsterdam: John Benjamins.

McCarthy, M. (2004). Lessons from the analysis of chunks. *The Language Teacher, 28*(7), 9–12.

McCarthy, M., & Carter, R. (1997). Written and spoken vocabulary. In N. Schmitt & M. McCarthy (Eds.), *Vocabulary: Description, acquisition and pedagogy* (pp. 20–39). Cambridge: Cambridge University Press.

McEnery, T., Xiao, R. (2005b). HELP or HELP to: What do corpora have to say? *English Studies, 86*, 161–187.

McEnery, T., Xiao, R., Tono, Y. (2006). *Corpus-based language studies: An advanced resource book.* New York, NY: Routledge.

Morley, D. (1994). *Television, audiences, and cultural studies.* New York, NY: Routledge.

Myers, G. (2001). "I'm out of it; You guys argue": Making an issue of it on The Jerry Springer Show. In A. Tolson (Ed.), *Television talk shows: Discourse, performance, spectacle* (pp. 173–191). Mahwah, NJ: Lawrence Erlbaum.

Oakes, M. P. (1998). *Statistics for corpus linguistics*. Edinburgh: Edinburg University Press.

Overstreet, M., & Yule, G. (1997). Locally contingent categorization in discourse. *Discourse Processes, 23*, 83–97.

Partington, A. (2004). "Utterly content in each other's company": Semantic prosody and semantic preference. *International Journal of Corpus Linguistics, 9*(1), 131–156.

Potter, W. J., & Smith, S. (2000). The contrast of graphic portrayals of television violence. *Journal of Broadcasting & Electronic Media, 44*(2), 301–323.

Prince, E., Bosk, C., & Frader, J. (1982). On hedging in physician-physician discourse. In J. di Pietro (Ed.), *Linguistics and the professions* (pp. 83–97). Norwood, NJ: Ablex.

Quaglio, P. (2002). *The language of NBC's Friends: Implications for ESL/EFL teaching and materials development*. Paper presented at the Fourth North American Symposium on Corpus Linguistics, Indianapolis, IN.

Quaglio, P., & Biber, D. (2006). The grammar of conversation. In A. McMahon & B. Aarts (Eds.), *The handbook of English linguistics* (pp. 692–723). Oxford: Blackwell.

Rayson, P., Berridge, D., & Francis, B. (2004). *Extending the Cochran rule for the comparison of word frequencies between corpora*. In 7th International Conference on Statistical analysis of textual data (JADT 2004), March 10–12, 2004, Louvain-la-Neuve, Belgium. Retrieved from http://eprints.comp.lancs.ac.uk/893 (July, 2007).

Rayson, P., & Garside, R. (2000). *Comparing corpora using frequency profiling*. In Workshop on Comparing Corpora, held in conjunction with the 38th annual meeting of the Association for Computational Linguistics (ACL 2000), October 1–8, 2000, Hong Kong. Retrived from http http://eprints.comp.lancs.ac.uk/344 (July, 2007).

Reppen, R. (1994). *Variation in elementary student writing*. Ph.D. Dissertation. Northern Arizona University.

Rey, J. M. (2001). Changing gender roles in popular culture: Dialogue in *Star Trek* episodes from 1966 to 1993. In S. Conrad & D. Biber (Eds.), *Variation in English: Multi-dimensional studies* (pp. 138 - 155). London: Longman.

Rühlemann, C. (2006). Coming to terms with conversational grammar: "Dislocation" and "dysfluency." *International Journal of Corpus Linguistics, 11*(4), 385–409.

Rühlemann, C. (2007). *Conversation in context: A corpus-driven approach*. London: Continuum.

Sbisa, Marina (2002). Speech acts in context. *Language & Communication, 22*, 421–436.

Schegloff, E., & Sacks, H. (1973). Opening up closings. *Semiotica, 8*, 289–327.

Schiffrin, D. (1987). *Discourse markers*. Cambridge: Cambridge University Press.

Scott, M. (1997). *WordSmith tools manual*. Oxford: Oxford University Press.

Signorielli, N. (2003). Prime-time violence 1993–2001: Has the picture really changed? *Journal of Broadcasting & Electronic Media, 47*(1), 36–57.

Smith, E. S. (1999). *Writing television sitcoms*. New York, NY: The Berkley Publishing Group.

Stenström, A.-B. (1991). Expletives in the London-Lund corpus. In K. Aijmer & B. Altenberg (Eds.), *English corpus linguistics: Studies in honour of Jan Svartvik* (pp. 239–253). London: Longman.

Stenström, A.-B., & Svartvik, J.(1994). Imparsable speech: Repeats and other nonfluencies in spoken English. In N. Oostdijk & P. de Haan (Eds.), *Corpus-based research into language: In honour of Jan Aarts* (pp. 241–254). Amsterdam: Rodopi.

Tagliamonte, S., & Roberts, C. (2005). So weird; so cool; so innovative: The use of intensifiers in the television series *Friends*. *American Speech, 80,* 280–300.

Tolson, A. (2001). Talking about talk: The academic debates. In A. Tolson (Ed.), *Television talk shows: Discourse, performance, spectacle* (pp. 7–30). Mahwah, NJ: Lawrence Erlbaum.

Tottie, G. (1991b). Conversational style in British and American English: The case of backchannels. In K. Aijmer & B. Altenberg (Eds.), *English corpus linguistics: Studies in honour of Jan Svartvik* (pp. 254–271). London: Longman.

Wachal, R. S. (2002). Taboo or not taboo: That is the question. *American Speech, 77,* 195–206.

Waksler, R. (2001). A new *all* in conversation. *American Speech, 76,* 128–138.

Wang, A. (2005). *When precision meets vagueness: A corpus-assisted approach to vagueness in Taiwanese and British courtrooms.* Paper presented at the 7th Biennial Conference on Forensic Linguistics/Language and Law. Cardiff University, UK.

Ward, G., & Birner, B. J. (1993). The semantics and pragmatics of *and everything. Journal of Pragmatics, 19,* 205–214.

Wardhaugh, R. (1985). *How conversation works.* Oxford: Basil Blackwell.

Washburn, G. (2001). Using situation comedies for pragmatic language teaching and learning. *TESOL Journal, 10,* 21–26.

White, M. (1994). *Language in job interviews: Differences relating to success and socioeconomic variables.* Unpublished Doctoral Dissertation. Northern Arizona University.

Wilson, D., & Sperber, D. (2002). Truthfulness and relevance. *Mind 111,* (443, July), 583–632.

Winzenburg, S. (2004). *TV's greatest sitcoms.* Baltimore, MD: PublishAmerica.

Wong, J. (2000a). Delayed next turn repair initiation in native-nonnative speaker English conversation. *Applied Linguistics, 21,* 244–267.

Woo, H. J., & Dominick, J. R. (2001). Daytime television talk shows and the cultivation effect among U.S. and international students. *Journal of Broadcasting & Electronic Media, 45,* 598–614.

Wood, H. (2001). "No, you rioted!": The pursuit of conflict in the management of "lay" and "expert" discourses on Kilroy. In A. Tolson (Ed.), *Television talk shows: Discourse, performance, spectacle* (pp. 65–87). Mahwah, NJ: Lawrence Erlbaum.

Yngve, V. H. (1970). On getting a word in edgewise. In *Papers from the sixth regional meeting, Chicago Linguistic Society* (pp. 567–578). Chicago, IL: Chicago Linguistic Society.

Appendix

Function	Category	Feature	Conversation		Friends		LL / Signif
			Raw Count	Normed	Raw Count	Normed	
Vague Language	Hedges	Kind of (like)	620	1051	541	895	7.55 **
		Sort of (like)	182	308	65	107	60.69 ****
	Coordin. tags	Or something (like that)	325	551	79	130	167.04 ****
		Or anything (like that)	63	107	28	46	14.71 ***
		(and) stuff (like that)	231	392	41	68	151.26 ****
	N of vague ref	Thing(s)	1499	2542	1379	2268	9.27 **
		Stuff	544	922	430	711	16.40 ****
		Shit	94	159	0	0	132.69 ****
	Disc. markers	You know	2648	4490	945	1563	883.97 ****
		I mean	1358	2303	1417	2343	0.21 N/S
	Stance markers	Probably	519	880	233	386	118.88 ****
		Perhaps	15	26	21	35	0.86 N/S
		Maybe	616	1044	823	1361	24.89 ****
	Modals	Could	1099	1863	1140	1886	0.07 N/S
		Might	328	556	204	337	32.38 ****

Function	Category	Feature	Conversation		Friends		LL / Signif
			Raw Count	Normed	Raw Count	Normed	
	Copular verbs	Seem	150	254	151	249	0.03 N/S
		Appear	3	5	4	7	0.12 N/S
	Utter. final	So	58	98	3	5	62.04 ****
	Intensifiers	Very	414	702	412	681	0.19 N/S
		So	496	842	876	1449	97.28 ****
		Really	2038	3456	2400	3968	21.15 *****
		Too	151	256	151	249	0.05 N/S
		Totally	106	180	243	402	51.86 ****
		Damn	29	49	31	51	0.03 N/S
	Disc markers	Oh	4702	7973	7746	12808	677.23 ****
		Wow	247	419	654	1081	180.57 ****
	Stance marker	Of course	112	190	226	374	36.40 ****
	Non-min. resp	Wow	77	130	54	90	4.66 *
		Sure	19	33	48	80	12.26 ***
		Fine	2	3	19	32	15.48 ****
	Expletives	Damn (overall)	57	97	115	190	18.51 ****
		Bastard	5	8	30	49	19.19 ****
		Bitch(y)	23	39	63	105	18.35 ****
		Son of a bitch	3.5	6	7	12	1.10 N/S
		Shit(ty)	144	244	0	0	203.28 ****
		Fuck (+ variations)	256	435	0	0	361.38 ****
		Ass (part of expres.)	29	49	69	115	15.82 ****

Emotional Language

Function	Category	Feature	Conversation		Friends		LL / Signif
			Raw Count	Normed	Raw Count	Normed	
	Innovations	Crap(py)	28	47	54	90	7.75 **
		All + adj /gerund	63	107	78	129	1.24 N/S
		Totally	6.5	11	19	32	6.09 *
	Lex. bundles	I can't believe (+ compl)	44	75	256	423	160.47 ****
		Thank you so much	1	2	56	93	67.57 ****
	Emphatic	Emphatic *do*	154	262	199	329	4.67 *
	Cop. verbs	Look	174	295	241	398	9.24 **
		Feel	112	190	173	286	11.67 ***
		Sound	82	139	124	205	7.60 **
	Slang	Suck	27	46	83	137	28.50 ****
		Piss(ed)(off)	26	44	8	13	10.49 **
		Screw(ed)(up)	19	32	42	69	8.32 **
		Freak out	12	20	98	162	74.53 ****
	Expletives	Damn (overall)	57	97	115	190	18.51 ****
		Bastard	5	8	30	49	19.19 ****
		Bitch(y)	23	39	63	105	18.32 ****
		Son of a bitch	3.5	6	7	12	1.10 N/S
		Shit(ty)	256	434	0	0	361.38 ****
		Fuck (+ variations)	144	244	0	0	203.28 ****
		Ass	38	65	115	191	38.66 ****
		Butt	20	34	79	130	36.14 ****
		Crap(py)	28	47	54	90	7.75 **

Informal Language

Function	Category	Feature	Conversation		Friends		LL / Signif
			Raw Count	Normed	Raw Count	Normed	
Slang		Piss(ed)(off)	26	44	8	13	10.49**
		Screw(ed)(up)	19	32	42	69	8.32**
		Suck	27	46	83	137	28.50****
		Check out	38	64	133	220	53.53****
		Hang out	27	46	95	157	38.46****
		Cool	156	264	233	385	13.46***
		Totally	6.5	11	19	32	6.09*
		What's up?	8	13	79	130	65.41****
		Freak (out)	12	20	98	162	74.53****
Vocatives		Guys	308	522	1090	1803	444.21****
		Man	106	180	343	568	125.77****
		Dude	17	29	114	188	78.06****
		Buddy	18	30	56	93	19.53****
		Folks	2	3	1	2	0.37 N/S
		Bro	2	3	2	3	0.00 N/S
		Bud	0	0	0	0	0.00 N/S
Innovations		All + adj/gerund	63	107	78	129	1.24 N/S
		So + (not) vb/n/					
		So + not + adj	2	3	42	70	43.72****
		In + neg pres perf + time	15	25	25	41	2.28 N/S
Semi-modals		e.g. going to, (had) better	4439	7527	5107	8445	31.47****
Repeats		e.g. I-I-I	2578	4372	4800	7937	624.89****
Greetings &		Hi	186	315	1271	2102	879.83****

Function	Category	Feature	Conversation		Friends		LL / Signif
			Raw Count	Normed	Raw Count	Normed	
	leave-takings	Hey	8	13.5	723	1195	907.33 ****
		Bye + bye-bye	153	259	320	529	56.12 ****
Narrativeness	Verb tense	Past tense	22003	37310	17614	29125	603.86 ****
	Pers. pronouns	3rd person pronouns	15549	26366	7091	11726	3454.4 ****
	Perfect aspect	Perfect aspect (overall)	1528	2591	1379	2280	11.86 ***
		Past perfect (overall)	203	344	72	119	68.35 ****
		Past perfect (can. funct)	192	326	37	61	118.84 ****
	Non-min resp	Mm/hmm/uh huh	1163	1973	80	132	1157 ****
		Okay	494	837	289	478	59.59 ****
		Right	178	302	31	52	118.0 ****
		Wow	77	130	54	90	4.66 *
Discourse Immediacy	Pers. pronouns	1st person pronouns	24141	40937	28593	47280	272.51 ***
		2nd person pronouns	1719	29150	23640	39090	22035.0****
	Vocatives	Overall	452	767	1607	2657	658.29 ****
	Greetings	Overall	193	328	1994	3297	1681.31****
	Leave-takings	Overall	153	259	320	529	56.12 ****

*   p < 0.05   critical value = 3.84
**   p < 0.01   critical value = 6.63
*** p < 0.001   critical value = 10.83
**** p < 0.0001 critical value = 15.13

Name index

Subject index

In the series *Studies in Corpus Linguistics (SCL)* the following titles have been published thus far or are scheduled for publication:

8   STENSTRÖM, Anna-Brita, Gisle ANDERSEN and Ingrid Kristine HASUND: Trends in Teenage Talk. Corpus compilation, analysis and findings. 2002. xii, 229 pp.

7   ALTENBERG, Bengt and Sylviane GRANGER (eds.): Lexis in Contrast. Corpus-based approaches. 2002. x, 339 pp.

6   TOGNINI-BONELLI, Elena: Corpus Linguistics at Work. 2001. xii, 224 pp.

5   GHADESSY, Mohsen, Alex HENRY and Robert L. ROSEBERRY (eds.): Small Corpus Studies and ELT. Theory and practice. 2001. xxiv, 420 pp.

4   HUNSTON, Susan and Gill FRANCIS: Pattern Grammar. A corpus-driven approach to the lexical grammar of English. 2000. xiv, 288 pp.

3   BOTLEY, Simon Philip and Tony McENERY (eds.): Corpus-based and Computational Approaches to Discourse Anaphora. 2000. vi, 258 pp.

2   PARTINGTON, Alan: Patterns and Meanings. Using corpora for English language research and teaching. 1998. x, 158 pp.

1   PEARSON, Jennifer: Terms in Context. 1998. xii, 246 pp.